Uneasy Rider

The story of my solo cross-country motorcycle adventure in the spring of 2006

Steven K. Cook

**This book is dedicate to
my wife Kathleen
"best of wives best of women"**

Check out my first attempt at writing a book:

Syzygy - The true story about my first oceanographic voyage in 1970 (written in 2014).
Available on Amazon.

Part I

Introduction:

First let me start off by saying that I don't mind being alone. Don't get me wrong, I like people a lot; I love women (especially the sweaty ones) and can tolerate most children (if they're interesting) most of the time. I think my not minding being alone can be traced back several decades to both my personal and professional lives. For most of my 35 professional years as an Oceanographer I was a "road warrior". I had to visit and support dozens of commercial container ships in most of our U. S. ports and several more outside of the US and I had to fly or drive and sometimes-even sail to do so. Even before, while growing up in California, I always had to drive long distances for various obligations. It seems then and now that I was always driving, flying or sailing somewhere. And while driving, flying or sailing somewhere, mostly driving I guess, I would find myself thinking about all sorts of things, just life in general, my life in particular, more sophisticated responses I should have used in past conversations when I had usually put my foot directly in my mouth and, of course, the Ice Ages (considering that we are only a bit of cosmic dust stuck between two Ice Ages). So you see, I sort of got used to being alone for long periods of time and looked at it as a bit of a blessing as it provide me the time to work out life's quandaries in my own mind. But I digress.

This is supposed to be a story about a solo cross-country motorcycle trip in the 60th year of my life. It wasn't supposed to be a solo trip, which by the way isn't really the smartest way one should attempt such a journey; but rather a 2 month long motorcycle odyssey, with a good friend, to visit the four geographical corners of the United States. We were going to drive the secondary and country roads whenever possible, camp out, visit those small out of the way historical or hysterical spots and, in general, just see all those places we hadn't ever seen and probably would never see again.

Well, the long and short of it was this. Even with more than a year of planning and setting a fixed departure date with which we both could agree, we were taken over by circumstances, which is, after all, life's way. Oh, we danced around this a bit trying to reschedule but it just didn't work out. If I was going to do this then I would do it alone. So, I decided to cut back on the adventure from doing the four geographical corners of the US to just a relatively quick coast-to-coast run. My reason for doing so is that I or I really should say we (my ever patient spouse and first wife Kathy and I) had already set aside the scheduled time for the motorcycle trip. I had to go now or just maybe I would never do it. Case closed.

Well, now that I didn't have to concern myself with any other personal coordination issues I was free to plan my own trip. Great! Now I could plan to stop and visit old friends, work colleagues, relatives if I was passing through their neck of the woods.

I should add, and it has been pointed out to me more than once and by more than one person that as a "control freak" this solo ride was the perfect scenario for me. I didn't have to worry about anyone other than myself. It was MY schedule. It was the perfect control situation. I could go when and where and as far as I wanted to or not. It was going to be MY choice. In my defense I must say that I really don't think I suffer from this "control freak" personality flaw; and if I do then I don't "suffer." Hogwash, I say, but if it works for this story, I'll agree to it just this once.

OK, so now I can plan the trip as I see fit. Here are the criteria I settled upon.

1. Follow the route of least precipitation.
2. Use secondary roads whenever possible and practical.
3. Stay in the least expensive "dirt bag" motels possible that are close to a source of beer and have cable TV (I needed the Weather Channel).
4. Eat at "Mom & Pop" type diners or restaurants whenever possible.
5. Don't push the ride, that is, stop when I get tired.

6. Don't tell anyone (friends, relatives or those that still owe me money or I them) that I was coming, until about 2 to 3 days away, so they wouldn't be waiting for me and conversely not have much time to run.

Note here that I settled on staying in motels rather than camping after making a fully loaded test ride up the coast prior to my departure. The facts are that my 1994 Harley Davidson FX Low Rider (aka Ruby) is just too small a bike to carry much stuff. So a camping tent, cooking and eating ware just didn't make the cut. In hindsight this was a good decision because at the close of the day after a long or even short ride, the last thing I really wanted to do was to set up a tent, boil some water and eat some backpacker food. What I want is a shower and a cold beer, maybe two. OK, OK three, but that's it!

The original plan was to depart on April 15, Tax Day and a day that I could remember even with short-term memory loss. But I didn't have to leave then; I could leave whenever I wanted, being the control freak that I am.

Around the time of April 15th I was monitoring our nation's weather and kept noticing that there were still snowstorms occurring in the Rocky Mountains and Dakotas. These late season storms contributed to severe thunderstorm and tornado activity throughout the Midwest and Texas. One of my original stops going east was to be Pagosa Springs, Colorado but as there was still inclement weather brewing up there, I decided to stop there on the West bound leg of the trip, later in the summer. So, I concentrated on watching the average daytime high temperature in El Paso, Texas and just as soon as that went above 60 degrees F. I would leave.

The temperature high in El Paso crept up ever so slowly. It struggled to reach my target daytime high of 60 degrees. Days went by and still no 60 degrees and I was beginning to have second thoughts. Finally on April 30th El Paso attained that magical 60 degrees and coincidently on May 1st a high-pressure area developed over the southwestern United States. I knew I could ride under that high for probably five days before it out ran out on me, but during those five days I should have pretty clear riding weather. Departure day was set for May 1st and the trepidation and fear began to gnaw at me. I had to get going or I wasn't going to go. Go I did.

One has to harden themselves for such a trip as this. Not just physically but psychologically as well. To say I wasn't nervous on departure day would be a lie. I guess that's why I stopped by Kathy's work to say goodbye one more time as I was leaving town; even after saying our goodbyes earlier that morning.

It was not without a bit of anxiety that I started this trip and by that I mean I was never ever really comfortable while riding and I'll tell you why.

Ruby, my "sled," my "ride," my "machine," my "bike," my " Harley" was a used bike. She had had two previous owners. She was a 1994 Harley Davidson FX Low Rider with an 80 cu. in. Evolution motor with **37,000** miles of use. She ran sweet, turned heads because of her good looks, and set off car alarms on parked cars along most any street; but Harley Davidson's do have a tendency to break down occasionally and that's OK if you are fairly close to home with a support network that can help you. If like me, you are riding the back roads of the US by yourself and where there is no cell phone coverage it gives you pause when you consider what all can go wrong. This feeling was exasperated even more when the previous owner mentioned to me that he had recently read an article in which it was said that this particular year and model had a tendency to throw a rod or rods at mileages above 37,000. The article went on to say that repairs were fairly easy and straightforward but you still needed a Harley dealer or mechanic to do the work. Ruby, being a Low Rider is also a fairly light bike in that it isn't as heavy as the Fat boys or Heritage models and as such "feels" the wind a lot more.

So, now my usual routine, no, actually my ever-constant routine while riding was as follows:

1. Check the left and right hand **M**irrors for any vehicles, but mostly big rigs, coming up behind me.
2. Check the left and right shoulders for **A**nimals.
3. Check the odometer to calculate the miles driven, as Ruby had no gas gauge, before looking for **G**as.
4. Check the **O**il pressure.

5. Check the **T**achometer.
6. Check the **S**peedometer.
7. Check the road in front of me for **S**topped traffic or folks making left hand turns in front of me while using cell phones.

Or **MAGOTS** for short.

In addition to the above list I was always cognizant of just how light Ruby is and
was constantly having to adjust (crab into) the cross winds and the pushing away by the bow wind wave and the sucking in of the stern wind wave of passing semi's and trailers.

Wait, what was that? Was it my front tire coming off or just a groove in the road or was it my back tire coming loose? What about that rattle, what's that? This was to be my constant routine for the next 8,000 miles. An "Uneasy Rider" was I.

On a more serious and sad note there are several folks, both friends and family, mentioned in this story that have since passed while I was writing this. This should be expected since I did this trip in 2006 and now it is 2019. A period of 13 years when some of my older relatives gave up waiting for this book. In a sense I can now say anything about them as I see fit and they cannot defend themselves. Too bad as I do tend toward exaggeration and occasionally stretch the truth.

The Journal

SOLO Coast to Coast to Coast-to-Coast Motorcycle Tour
May 1 to June 11, 2006

May 1, 2006 - Cardiff, CA to Gila Bend, AZ 317 miles

Departed Cardiff about 8:30 AM after saying goodbye to my neighbors that were out in the front yards when I started Ruby. Stopped by the Kraken, my local watering hole next to the Pacific Ocean for a photo op. Stopped by Cubic Corp. to say one last goodbye to Kathy and another photo op and then headed east.

Final goodbye to Kathy at Cubic in San Diego, California (Pacific Ocean start)

Stopped at Buckman Springs Rest stop for my first rest and water break. Took State Route 98 (old road) from Ocotillo to just east of Calexico. Filled gas tank and stomach in Calexico but couldn't take route 98 very much further east due to construction. So, jumped back up on I-8 and continued east. Stopped at the Dunes rest stop just west of Yuma to stretch my legs.

At first everything was OK, as I was riding east on I-8 with which I was very familiar. Even when I left I-8 at Ocotillo and headed southeast on SR-89 toward Mexicali I was still OK because I had ridden this road before. It was after Mexicali, after I had stopped for gas and a burrito that I almost dropped Ruby and I found myself shaking as I fought to keep her upright.

Why was I shaking? It almost felt like an adrenalin let down. Like, so far, I had been riding on pure adrenalin and stopping in unfamiliar territory had finally caught up to me and realized that I was now on my own.

After the shaking passed I continued to head east. I had to get back up on I-8 because SR-89 was closed east of Mexicali. I rode to Yuma, Arizona and planned to take a photo of me and Ruby in front of the "Welcome to Arizona" sign, but there was no place to park to do so. Oh well, I kept riding and continued on toward Gila Bend. By now the temperature was well about 100 degrees and I was looking forward to the afternoon cooling. So far so good!

I was, unknowingly, just five miles short of Gila Bend, Arizona when Ruby starting coughing and sputtering. I quickly turned the gas reserve valve on and then Ruby completely stopped. I was out of gas! I pulled off on the shoulder to check if I had turned the petcock valve in the wrong direction? I dismounted and looked closely at the valve and determined that I had turned it correctly. I climbed back on and tried starting Ruby again. No happiness. So I exercised the valve a bit by turning it back and forth through its range of movement and shook Ruby to see if I could splash some remaining gas into the petcock, but heard no splashing sound from the tank. Not a good sign but I tried starting her again. Again, no happiness. Shit! Did I mention that the temperature was well over 100 degrees and I was wearing all my designer black leather? Did I also mention that there was no cell phone signal out there?

I didn't exactly know how far I was from Gila Bend and there was no exit ramp that I could see in front of me but there was one behind me about a mile back. I remembered this because the sign had read "No services". It was just a farm road with some migrant housing next to the freeway. I figured there might be a phone there that I could use if I knocked on the right door.

I couldn't just leave Ruby there along side of the freeway with all my stuff strapped to her so I turned her around and started walking her back toward the off ramp I had just passed. I hadn't walked a 100 feet when a fellow by the name of Brent driving a diesel powered pick up truck pulled over and asked if I needed some help. Brent may drive a diesel powered pick up truck but he also carries a one-gallon can of gas in the bed of that truck. Brent, a Harley rider himself, said that he always stops for Harley riders, cute girls and, yes, grudgingly little old ladies. He gave me his gas! Brent followed me into Gila Bend and wouldn't pull into the gas station I stopped at to let me refill his gallon can of gas. He just waved as he drove on by. I've always said that God watches over drunks and fools. This fool should have filled up in Yuma. Thank you Brent, I'll pass this help along to someone else when the time presents itself.

So after the adrenalin shakes in Mexicali and the embarrassment of walking Ruby against traffic on I-8 I decided that I would just stay the night in Gila Bend and start fresh tomorrow. I needed a beer anyway!

After this little incident I began looking for gas whenever I passed 100 miles of riding. Even though Ruby should be able to cover about 160 miles on a single tank of gas I never violated this personal rule again for the entire trip. Ruby had no gas gauge so I monitored the odometer to determine when I had passed 100 miles. Also, as this was the second time Ruby's reserve tank failed to function properly I decided that I would replace the petcock valve.

Stayed at the El Coronado motel for $35.00 because it was within walking distance to a beer source. All night, both westbound and eastbound freight trains rolled through Gila Bend, none with the intention of stopping. Their crescendowring sound accentuated by the haunting sounds of the whistles made for an interesting reflection of times past. I was glad I had turned off the AC and opened the window.

Will head for Tombstone tomorrow.

Notice the cowboy grilling out of the back of his truck at the El Coronado Motel in Gila Bend, Arizona.

May 2, 2006 - Gila Bend, AZ to Columbus, NM 397 miles

Departed Gila Bend at 6:30 AM and rode to Casa Grande and stopped for breakfast at The Cookie Jar and gassed up too. From now on when I pass 100 miles I start looking for a gas station. I'm not running out again. Besides with my luck Brent would probably stop again to save me and how embarrassing would that be?

Took the scenic route off I-10 onto US-80 south down through Tombstone, Bisbee and Douglas AZ following basically the same route my parents did back in 1956 when we drove from San Diego to Eureka KS for a family Christmas visit. Tombstone is over 5000 feet in elevation and I had forgotten just how high and bleak that part of the desert is and how cold it can be, even in the summer time.

Outskirts of Tombstone, Arizona

Continued on US-80 as it turned north past Apache (where Geronimo finally surrendered) to Rodeo NM where I turned east on State Route 9. SR-9 parallels the US & Mexico border most of the way across New Mexico and crossed over the continental divide. It is a very secondary rode. No traffic, except lots of Border Patrol vehicles but they were off the road and cruising the shoulders, no cell phone coverage, no gas and no motels, no nothing!

Finally found a small hotel in Columbus, about half way across New Mexico named Hacienda de Villa for $45.00. The owners recommended dinner in Mexico just 3 miles south. This is the area that Pancho Villa terrorized back in his day. In 1916 Pancho Villa and his raiders attacked

Columbus, NM and killed 18 Americans. I guess Pancho had some issues with the US back then. Until "Lefty" dropped a dime on him.

Hacienda de Villa, Columbus, New Mexico

Had a nice Mexican food dinner and a couple of beers and got back to the motel just past dusk. No traffic on any of the roads, no people walking the streets; just one light on over the door of a bowling alley about two blocks from my "Hacienda". Walked over to check it out and found out it was the only show in town. There must have been seven or eight people in there. Thankfully, they did sell beer. Texas tomorrow.

May 3, 2006 - Columbus, NM to Marathon, TX 332 miles

What a great day today was. Got underway 7:30 AM and finally got to El Paso about 9:00 AM. It was cold enough for me to stop and put on my leather jacket. The sun was behind the clouds and it was cold. There was absolutely no one on this SR-9 Road. I would ride at 70 mph and wouldn't see another car or truck for almost an hour and then it was usually an old pick up truck being driven by a Hispanic with every seat filled up with his family. They always would wave at me. They may have been shocked at seeing a single Harley rider so far out in the boon docks. Routes like this are really pleasant to drive but it does give one pause if something should break on the bike. It would be a long hike to help. As such my mind was constantly busy as I continually checked my MAGOTS. In fact this was my standard drill every day I rode which was tedious at best and most of all fatiguing; but I left no room for complacence.

While riding through El Paso, which now seems the size of Los Angeles, a fellow in a Volkswagen Jetta beeped his horn and gave me the "thumbs up" sign. Ruby still turns heads. What more can one man ask from his Harley; except that it keeps running as good as it has so far.

Got off I-10 at Van Horn TX to catch US-90 heading south and east and found a Mexican restaurant named Chuys that the football coach/TV announcer John Madden had discovered and talked up on Monday Night Football. It was a great little place serving Texas style Mexican food and worth visiting again. I then headed south on US-90, into the Lobo Valley.

Chuy's Mexican Restaurant in Van Horn, Texas

Bleak, bleak, bleak. They grow a lot of Pecans in that Lobo Valley. I guess Pecans thrive in bleak. US-90 in this part of the world is another class A secondary road. By class A I mean you can literally drive for hours and see only three or four vehicles.

It was a bit windy today and some gusts really "puckered" me up and got my attention. I saw a large Dust Devil coming across the road in my direction. I just had time to brace myself and the bike before driving through the wind shear. A real thrill! I did a lot of crabbing that day. This can be fatiguing after a while. I also found toward the end of the day I seemed to go slower. My throttle hand gets tired and droops down so the result is to go slower. There were no cruise controls or highway bars (foot rests) on Ruby.

Passed through the town of Marfa which advertised their must see attraction they call "Marfa's Mysterious Lights". Evidently Marfa must be in competition with Roswell, NM for alien sightings. A little farther along US-90 I passed a sign that said the movie "Giant" was filmed in this area.

Saw plenty of skunk and rabbit road kill today. Seems as if west Texas could use a few more raptors. Also saw many Pronghorn Antelope and large Mule Deer. Although I guess all deer look large when laying dead and bloated along side the road.

Stopped for gas and a water break in a town about 40 miles north of Marathon and asked the clerk if she new if the next town south (Marathon) had a motel or not. She said yes, the Gauge Hotel, which is supposed to be a historical landmark. I asked if there was a motel in the next town south of Marathon and she didn't know, as she had never been there! It was getting late in the afternoon and so I decided that I had better go with sure thing of the Gauge Hotel in Marathon and not chance there being no motel in the small town south of Marathon.

I was able to hear a voice mail from my cousin Jeannie Price today but with such limited cell coverage my answer will have to wait until sometime tomorrow. I know that Kathy will be a bit concerned with not hearing from me, but she was to expect occasional blank zones like this. Tomorrow both Kathy and Jeannie will, hopefully, hear from me.

I was cresting a grade just north of Marathon when I spotted a freight train lumbering up the same grade from the opposite direction and about an 1/8," mile to the west of me. The late afternoon shadows were lengthening and the train and I were the only ones around so, in case the engineer was watching, I raised my arm in a salute to the him and his train and he responded in kind with several bursts from his train whistle. Two travelers each locked in their own ways to a fixed path and journey. One of us on a steel track and the other on an asphalt track and both traveling in opposite directions; a sign of mutual respect for those travelers that are trapped by their own design. Only flying could free us more but it is so difficult to wave to each other when flying. That train whistle gave me goose bumps that I carried on my skin for the next few miles. And to this day, in my mind, whenever I revisit that time and place!

Finally stopped in Marathon, TX about 4:00 PM local time and having crossed another time zone and loosing another hour. I elected not to stay at the "tricked out," historical and expensive Gauge Hotel but rather at the Marathon Motel located on the edge of town. It looked similar to the Gauge Hotel in that they used the same color stucco in its construction. Their room rates started at $70.00 but I talked my way into one of their derelict rooms for $45.00. Score! The clerk said I made a good decision to stay there but suggested I visit the Gauge Hotel to check out the White Buffalo Bar. She said it was pricey but worth the visit. Not being one that easily turns down checking out a new and historical bar, I did. The local Pale Ale was $3.00 a pint so not so pricey. Took some photos of me standing in front of the White Buffalo head mounted on the wall which I was told was worth more than the bar itself. Apparently this is truly a white buffalo and not an albino specimen. Very rare in nature but it does occasionally occur.

The "White Buffalo" inside the White Buffalo Bar in Marathon, Texas

Little did I realize that twelve years after my visit to the Gauge Hotel Anthony Bourdain's TV show <u>Parts Unknown</u> would film an episode there.

After a couple of pints of the local Pale Ale I stopped at the local grocery store to pick up a pre made sandwich and a couple of beers for dinner. The problem was that in Marathon they don't sell single beers. You have to buy a whole six pack. I didn't want a whole six-pack, as I couldn't carry any leftovers on the bike the next day. I just wanted a sandwich and beer and sit on the front porch of my derelict casita and watch the sunset.

A local volunteer fireman overheard my conversation with the store clerk (who he was trying to persuade to come visit him) about my beer issue and, with a typical volunteer mind set, offered to by some beer for himself and give me a couple from his purchase, just as long as it was Coors Light. Being the well-traveled diplomat that I am I said "Hell yes, I love Coors Light". Another "good" man I've met on this trip and he wouldn't take my money for the beers. He said, "In Marathon we share beers all the time".

So I returned to my casita as the sun was about to set, sat on the front porch, ate my sandwich and drank the beers while listening to the wind-mill powered water pump tower, the passing freight trains and watching the quail and doves play in the dust in the yard in front of my ramshackle room. Life is good!

Marathon Motel, Marathon, Texas

     Goal tomorrow is Hondo, TX, but the weather looks a bit "wet". I asked the motel clerk what she thought about tomorrows weather and she said not to worry. We'll see.

May 4, 2006 - Marathon, TX to Sequin, TX 369 miles

Departed Marathon about 7:15 AM after walking Ruby down to the main road so as not to awaken any guests when I fired her off. The day looked threatening with lots of tropical looking clouds thick enough to provide for a great sunrise but also cold enough to force me to don my leather jacket to fend off the chill.

As I pulled out of the Marathon Motel and rode past the Gauge Hotel, I noticed standing in front of the old hotel a fellow I had met the previous night at the White Buffalo Bar and who was staying at the Gauge Hotel. This fellow along with his wife were riding a full dress Honda and pulling a bike trailer with an additional storage pod on top of the trailer. He told me during our previous night's conversation that he was 64 years old and had been riding for only two years. He told a story about how he dropped his bike and trailer and how righting it took all the strength he could muster and that he was still sore from doing so. He also told me that the trailer he was pulling popped up into a sleeping tent! Who knew? Too much rig for me and I was glad to be traveling light and fast. We waved to each other as I rode by. I wonder if he was a bit envious of Ruby and my light load?

The clouds in conjunction with my dark riding goggles made easy identification of the deer standing along side the highway difficult. There were so many road kills along that stretch of US-90 down to Del Rio that I was nervous and constantly scanning both sides of the road for animals. I was worried that the noise of Ruby would startle them into jumping. The worry was which way would they jump? Off the highway or onto it?

Wind picked up early this morning which made riding tough and with the animal threat so large I had to keep my speed down to about 55 mph for most of the day. The reduced speed just added to the positive effect of the great vistas and plateaus along this part of Texas. Spotted many deer standing along the side of the road and was very glad they all stayed where they were. Also saw wild goats, bison and peccary today. There are several large private hunting ranches out this way. I believe it was in this area that Vice President Cheney accidentally shot and wounded one of his cronies while dove hunting.

23

Today I crossed over the Pecos River just upstream from where it runs into the Rio Grand River. The Pecos comes up suddenly and from out of nowhere. Nothing but bleak high desert then all of sudden you're on a bridge 200 feet over the Pecos River gorge. What a pleasant surprise this turned out to be.

Pecos River where it flows into the Rio Grande River, Texas

Also passed Judge Roy Bean's place. Judge Roy Bean was known as the "Hanging Judge" back in his day. He was the territorial law in that part of Texas that required him to ride a "circuit" passing out judicial decisions in many a small town. His philosophy was not to delay his judgments and his decisions were usually fast and fatal. Didn't stop to visit the museum but will when Kathy and I retrace this trip after she retires.

Finally turned east on US-90 at Del Rio Texas and the truck traffic really picked up. The route between San Antonio to Del Rio and then into Mexico handles a bunch of NAFTA commerce.

Stopped in Hondo, TX for Barbecue and to give John Brucks (an old work colleague and friend) a call. John is from Hondo and his family still has a ranch there. I didn't want to ride by and miss him if he and, his wife, Lanelle were in Hondo visiting. Turned out they weren't in Hondo at that time which gave me the excuse to stay with them when I passed through Mississippi.

McBee's Bar-B-Q Restaurant in Hondo, Texas

The wind had died down a bit and US-90 turned into a two-lane road in both directions and I was able to make good time all the way to San Antonio and was just able to avoid the peak of rush hour traffic.

I stopped at a rest stop and met an old (my age) Viet Nam era biker who regaled me with lots of stories about Texas biker gangs. According to him most are just "pussies," but I should be watchful anyway. One never knows when you're going to run into a burnt out "conspiracy theorist" with an agenda. I love it!

Pushed on to Sequin, TX and stayed at an Americas Best Value Inn and Suites for $49.00. Should make it to cousin Jennie and Yoli's place in Fulshear tomorrow.

May 5, 2006 - Sequin, TX to Fulshear, TX   139 miles

Short day today just to get over to cousin Jeannie and her adopted daughter, Yoli's, new place in Fulshear. Hit a little rain shower and had to stop and put on my rain gear. It was only a brief squall and I soon had to stop and remove the gear, as it was just too hot to keep it on.

Saw a train accident today somewhere near Columbus, TX. Seems as if a tractor trailer carrying either feed or fertilizer tried to cross over a train crossing in front of an Amtrak passenger train. I don't think anyone was hurt as the tractor had made it over the tracks and was still upright but the trailer was scattered down the track for about 100 yards. The nose of the Amtrak engine was scratched up a lot but the train was still on the tracks. There was absolutely no place to pull over and park or I would have taken a photo.

Got off the I-10/US-90 east highways at Seely in search of Country Route 1093 which is the road that leads to Jeannie's place. The clerk at the 7/11 store was absolutely clueless as to where this CR-1093 was or even where his store was located. This I learned after waiting several minutes for him to finish a personal cell phone call on which he was focused. It turned out that CR-1093 was the very next intersection down from his store. This and the earlier incident in Texas where a clerk had never been to the town just 60 miles away causes me some concern about the geographical knowledge, or lack thereof, of a lot of our populace.

Arrived at Jeannie's and Yoli's about noon and she had a big brunch prepared. House smelled great and is very pretty. She always makes you feel comfortable. After lunch we all went shopping to Sam's Club to pick up some picnic items for Jeannie's Church Social on Sunday. Also stopped at Kroger's to pick up some items for dinner on Saturday plus some cleaning items for Ruby and my leather chaps.

Jeannie and Yoli Price in Fulshear Texas

Jeannie wants me to marinade and cook a Tri-Tip roast and reduce the marinade to a sauce. She remembers enjoying a similar menu at our house sometime in the past. I hope I can do this to her liking as I usually "wing" this type of activity based on my spice craving for the day and my level of inebriation while cooking.

Upon returning from our shopping spree Yoli retrieved the mail and it contained a card and letter from Kathy. Only took two days to get here from Cardiff. What a nice surprise. Kathy usually slips a card into my suitcase or briefcase most times when I traveled. I almost always forget she does this and I sometimes don't find the cards until just before returning home. She did the same this time in my saddlebags but now she has trumped this by having mail waiting for me when I arrived at Jennie's.

Jeannie cooked a great Chicken Cacciatore and we drank a bottle of Chianti I picked up while shopping. Finished my laundry and Jeannie even ironed my shirts for me! During the laundry process I thought I lost my face scarf and Jeannie replaced it with another scarf in the form of the state of Texas "Lone Star" flag. Very appropriate and I'll be sure to wear it, especially while south of the Mason-Dixon Line. Just to be polite and not expecting a "yes" answer, I asked Jeannie if there was anything she needed done around the house with which I could help. Always trying to be helpful I am. I should have kept my mouth shut. Her list began with cutting up a downed tree that fell in her front yard during the last thunderstorm. She had a chain saw but it hadn't been started in over a year. There was no chain oil or gas/oil mixture for fuel. I did manage to get it started and a few cuts made before running out of fuel. Tomorrow we'll have to go to a hardware store to get the aforementioned items as well as a Rat-tail file so I can sharpen the chain. Her mop needed repair and I was able to accomplish that OK. She also wanted her rain gutters cleaned out of accumulated pine needle mulch before the expected rain tomorrow. The problem is that she can't climb up a ladder and the pine mulch has become home for colonies of fire ants. Wear gloves and work fast was the order of business. I was able to accomplish this with minimal trauma and fire ant bites.

Jeannie and Yoli have a new pup named "Sue Ann" from the Dallas TV series. Sun Ann was a hurricane Katrina survivor dog they found at the pound. She seems to be part hound and is sharp as a tack. She is about one year old, so still a pup and active as hell. Of course, neither Yoli nor Jeannie know anything about training a dog so there are many "accidents". So, I expect it will be a long training process with Sue Ann. I got up early and took Sue Ann outside and we both pissed in the grass. After fewer than two tries she now sits on command and will even do it on her own when she wants your attention. This is a smart dog and it is too bad that she will forever be an "inside" animal.

This was an R&R day at Jeannie's. I had a chance to clean Ruby and make some downstream calls. Jeannie had an old book I would like to find:

Pictorial History of the Wild West
By James D. Horan & Paul Sam
Crown Publisher, Inc. NY
Copy-write 1954
Sixth Printing 1961

Cooked the Tri-Tip and made a beef salad with no sauce. Watched lots of HBO, lots of HBO. Aside from the foo foo coffee cup and bedspread it was a very pleasant visit but I was eager to move on. Next target was to visit Jim Nelson, an old National Weather Service, work colleague in League City TX.

On a sad note, since I made this trip, little Yoli has since passed away. We all miss her, as she was such a sweet girl.

May 7, 2006 - Fulshear, TX to Galveston, TX   120 miles

Another short day as some time was used up in locating a Harley dealership in Houston (closed on Sundays and Mondays). I wanted to change the oil and check the front break. The front break isn't stopping as quickly as it should and it squeaks a bit. But, alas, it will have to wait.

Headed south on US-45 and located Jim & Betty Nelson's (an old work colleague from my National Oceanic and Atmospheric Administration days) home but they weren't there. I could tell that it was the Nelson's home as there was a plaque on the door that said so and I heard the barking of their wiener dog inside. So I left a note. I couldn't find Jim's telephone number in any local books and his old numbers that I had were never answered or were disconnected.

Thunderstorms were to the east of me and I could either return north up US-45 to I-10 then turn east or continue south on US-45 to Galveston and possibly skirt the storms. I decided to head south as the clouds looked less threatening that way and it would give me the opportunity to see the Gulf of Mexico again and could make this trip a "coast to coast to coast trip." So much for less threatening clouds. I got about half way to Galveston when I rode into my first serious rain. I got off the highway and hid out under an overpass for about ½ an hour fighting off the mosquitoes. After the squall passed over I continued south, passing through two more rain cells, to Galveston and the Poop Deck Club where, in the past, I had spent a lot of time waiting for the Gulf of Mexico to calm down. Several years ago a work colleague and I were tasked to do some ocean circulation work in the Buccaneer Oilfield just offshore of this particular part of the coast and we made Galveston and the Poop Deck Bar our base of operations.

The Poop Deck Bar in Galveston, Texas (Gulf of Mexico)

By the time I got to Galveston I had decided to stay and avoid the late afternoon heat and humidity on the long run from here up to Beaumont, TX. So I rode into old Galveston to visit some of the old haunts there. This part of Galveston used to be the center of entertainment back in the day. Many a popular act came to Galveston to perform in the various clubs that were thriving then. Galveston had "speakeasie's," fashionable restaurants and regular folks' eateries too. When I was there only a few were left, like the "Old Galveston Club" (converted from a speakeasy to a legit bar now), "Apache Tortilla Factory" (an old school Mexican restaurant) and "Sole Bones" (a barbecue place with the catch line "You can beat our prices but you can't beat our meat)."

The bartender (I think his name was Felix) at the Old Galveston Club was in his late sixties with a full head of silver white hair and he told us the story of how the first Margarita was concocted. It seems that Peggy Lee was one of the entertainers who used to star in some of the Galveston nightclubs. One night she and a few of her friends came in and as she didn't drink much she asked Felix if he would make her something that didn't taste like liquor. So Felix came up with a drink using Tequila, Triple Sec and Lime juice and coated the glass rim with sugar to sweeten it. It was later on that folks started coating the glass with salt, perhaps as a nod toward tradition with Tequila.

Old Galveston was a bit industrial with grain silos loaded with corn, wheat or soy beans waiting to be loaded on ships for delivery elsewhere. These were known to occasionally and spontaneously explode which, as you might imagine, had a negative impact on the surrounding area. As is in most industrial seaports the area was amply served by many small local bars to handle the noon lunch and after work "happy hour" crowds.

Soon after arriving in the late afternoon I went looking for my "old Galveston" and found one of those local bars. It was between lunch and happy hour and there were very few people around so I thought it would a good time to grab a beer before finding lodging for the night.

I parked Ruby at the curb and entered a rather small and dark bar that I don't remember ever having visited. As I walked in and put my goggles, and gloves on the bar an old "Mama San" standing about half way down the bar in a space that opened up from behind the bar motioned to me that I should sit down there. By old "Mama San" I mean she looked about 50, which means she was probably closer to 60. It was her bar so I abided by her request and took the closest bar stool to where she was standing. I assumed she just didn't want to walk to where I first started to sit. I asked for the closest and coldest beer she had. She brought it, a Lone Star as I recall. As I was taking my first long pull on my cold Lone Star she stepped from behind the bar and up between my legs and started fumbling with the buckles on my riding chaps and jeans. As was usual with my life up to that time when faced with a dicey situation I usually resorted to humor or speed to free myself. I wasn't as fast as I used to be and I had just started that beer, so I opted for the humor approach. I grabbed my Mama San by the shoulders and held her off at arms length and with a polite smile on my face asked her if "she wasn't a bit old for this kinda shit?" I swear her response was almost straight out of the movie

Full Metal Jacket. She didn't say "beaucoup boom boom, me love you long time" but rather "me fuck you real good." So I gently spun her around by her shoulders nudged her back behind the bar. As I did this, with her back to me, she hiked her dress up over her shoulders showing me that she was not wearing a stitch of underwear and then turned around and presented her front to me, which displayed a rather well groomed pubic area. As I recall her rather sparse pubic hair was trimmed like an arrowhead pointed south.

About this time another customer walked in the front door and the Mama San lowered her dress. He took a quick look around and probably thought he was at the end of the line then left. I guessed he might have been a local, as he didn't seem too surprised by the scene unfolding in front of him. I took another long pull from my beer and in my most inquisitive voice asked my Mama San just how she did this when this was a public bar? She informed me she would lock the front door and climb up on a pool table to service her customer. I thought that was a rather resourceful solution on her part, told her so and took another long pull of my beer and made a mental note not to every play pool in this place.

I told her that I appreciated her attention but that I didn't feel like playing any pool and I first had to find lodging and food after having ridden from west of Houston in the heat and humidity. I took the last pull on my beer and hurriedly left. Funny, I don't remember these dive bars being quite this friendly back in the day!

Later on that afternoon after getting cleaned up I rode back downtown to get some dinner and noticed the open sign on in the window of my Mama San's bar and a customer trying repeatedly to open the door. Apparently the door was locked.

I figured I could make it to Carriere, MS by tomorrow if the weather holds. It will be a long day but doable. Received a voice mail from my cousin Jodie Cook in Highlands, NC offering to let me stay at their home in Highlands. Good news! Also, got a call from Jim Nelson. They had been to church and I did have an old number.

Stayed at a Motel 9 for $47.00 and grabbed a sandwich at a seafood place on the corner.

34

May 8, 2006 - Galveston, TX to Carriere, MS   372 miles

A good day today even though it broke this morning with a drizzle that I thought would define the day but it didn't. Departed Galveston about 7:00 AM and took the Bolivar Ferry across the mouth of Galveston Bay and headed east on SR-57 until I couldn't go any further because of road closures due to hurricane Katrina damage.

Crossing Galveston Bay on the Bolivar Ferry in Galveston, Texas

I am now entering that area of Katrina damage that extends all the way from here to Pascagoula Mississippi. So I had to turn north on SR-124 toward Beaumont, TX where I would hook up with I-10 again headed east. There was lots of road and other infrastructure damage along SR-124.

Merged onto I-10 at Beaumont, TX and headed east. Finally got out of Texas (home of the big dually pickup truck) and into Louisiana (Sportsman's Paradise and home of the Armadillo Road Kill) and this is where I-10 turned to shit. I felt like I was on a ski slalom racecourse as I dodged pothole after pothole, some so deep I could crash Ruby if I had hit them straight on. So far this is the roughest road I've had to ride since leaving San Diego. There was no wind and I made good time. I stopped in Iowa, LA for gas and had some "Boudin (pronounced Boodan) Balls". Having never heard of Boudin Balls I had to try this local delicacy. They are a meat/rice filled sausage casing that is battered and deep fat fried. When you bite into them the grease squirts out the side of the ball. Almost palatable when liberally doused with hot sauce. Welcome to the South!

Crossed over the Mississippi River at Baton Rouge and later stopped in Slidell to look for postcards to send home. I promised the Kraken crew that I would send them a postcard when I crossed the Mississippi River. No luck finding postcards in Slidell.

Arrived at John (an old National Marine Fisheries Service work colleague and friend from my Miami days) and Lanelle Brucks place in Hideaway Lakes about 3:00 PM. Their house still looks great even though there is still lots of hurricane damage as the eye of Katrina came directly over Hideaway Lakes. They were able to take advantage of a private traveling tree removal crews that had come down from up north just to make gobs of cash from folks that needed help right now. It took weeks to finally clear the road all the way around Hideaway Lakes. It was a good thing that John and Lanelle's place was so close to the front of the development.

John and Lanelle are still the perfect hosts and make one feel right at home. Lanelle had to visit her mother who had recently entered a nursing home after which she had a bowling gig so John and I had a couple of Black Jack's and met Lanelle later for dinner. Fried catfish, Gumbo, two pounds of crawdads and a couple of beers later we were back home BS'ing and watching 24 on TV. We had stopped and found a place that sold postcards so now I can write Kathy, Jet, Colin, and the Kraken. After that I hit the wall and called it off. Tornado watch and warnings just to the north of us kept our interest for a while and I told John that if Ruby was blown over by morning that he would have to help me pick her up.

John and Lanelle Brucks in Carriere, Mississippi

Morning broke cloudy and a bit wet. I sat at John and Lanelle's kitchen counter drinking coffee and watching a family of Canadian Geese and local ducks work the lake. I listened to the birds chirping and saw a goose, gander and five goslings paddle across the cove and climb out to feed on John and Lanelle's backyard grass. The Brucks have a very nice spot here. John and Lanelle's place is as comfortable as an old friends place up on Cabosacontee Lake in Maine. I guess just having a view of the water has a calming effect on me.

Today's agenda is to clean Ruby, do laundry writ emails, contact my cousin Jodie in Highlands, NC and get final directions to his place; I'll also call Frank and Mary-Ann Hebard (another work colleague and friend and the man who first hired me for NOAA) warning them that I was headed their way. Also need to watch the Weather Channel, which is now becoming a mandatory exercise. All those storms I avoided by going south along the Mexican border and as far south as Galveston have finally caught up to me. They continue to form and cross over mid Texas, suck up heat and moisture from the Gulf of Mexico, finally impacting against the Appalachian Mountain system as severe thunderstorms and tornados!

May 10, 2006 - Carriere, MS to Tuscaloosa, AL 243 miles

Got underway at 7:30 AM. It was a great visit with John and Lanelle.
I started off following US-11 that basically parallels I-59 all the way to
Virginia trying to keep to my plan of using secondary roads instead of
interstates as much as possible. It didn't take me long (only about 45 minutes)
to determine that following secondary roads east of the Mississippi is much
different than the secondary roads west of the Mississippi. First of all the
towns are much closer together so you are constantly having to slow down to
obey the local traffic laws and secondly, there is a lot more traffic on these
secondary roads. Traffic like school buses, commuters and farm vehicles.
Most of which seemed to require making left hand turns against oncoming
traffic and basically stopping the traffic behind them, mainly Ruby and me. I
wasn't making much progress and I needed to get as far north and east as fast
as I could, especially during these morning hours to avoid those afternoon
thunderstorms. So I quit US-11 and jumped up on I-59 where I could make
some time. It was still early on I-59 and the wind and traffic were light and
the road was good.

The clouds expectedly kept increasing as the day progressed and my
idea of skirting to the southeast of the approaching weather was rapidly
running out of time. The line of thunderstorms caught up to me at Foster, AL
and 10 miles short of Tuscaloosa. Rain and hail came down in torrents and it
came on so fast I had no time to stop and put on my rain gear. I got off I-59
and headed west about a mile to a gas station and the Foster General Store
where I could ride out the weather. By the time I got there the road was a
river, the visibility had decreased to less than 100 feet and the lightening was
striking the ground within sight and smell.

I hung out at the Foster General Store for about an hour and a half
basically drip-drying and making small talk with the owner and clerk behind
the counter. It was also a bit disconcerting to be standing there in rain soaked
leather garb with a California Harley Davidson parked outside next to a
pickup truck with a fully loaded gun rack displayed in the rear window and
bumper stickers reading "Liberalism is a disease" and "Sportsman for GW

39

Bush." It never really stopped raining, but after a while we could at least see across the street. It was then that the owner who had been listening to the weather channel on his radio said "This is the lull between the front that just passed over us and the next one coming along within an hour". If I was going to make a break for Tuscaloosa I had better do it now and I did.

Outside the Foster General Store in Foster, Alabama

I found a Motel 8 ($45.00) in Tuscaloosa that had a laundromat right next door. As soon as I was in the room I turned on the Weather Channel and there was Tuscaloosa exactly between the front that slammed me and the next one coming down the line. I used every coat hanger in the room to spread out my wet leathers to dry and laid other smaller items across every lamp. Then I went next door to avail myself of the use of that laundromat to properly dry the clothes I had been wearing.

Weather Channel showing the thunderstorm band that hit me (orange lower right) and the one I managed to miss (orange upper left) by stopping in Tuscaloosa, Alabama

Tomorrow is supposed to be clear so I might make it to Highlands, NC if I can get an early start.

May 11, 2006 - Tuscaloosa, AL to Blueridge, GA 302 miles

Hard day today! The morning broke in a clearing mode but it was cold and cloudy all day. I guess I'm on the backside (colder side) of that front that passed through yesterday. That makes sense. Got rained on twice which was a bitch. Lots of wind buffeting which kept my speed down plus lots of truck traffic.

Finally got off the Interstate after looping up to Chattanooga and then back down into Georgia and onto SR-2 towards Highlands (I thought). Turns out that SR-2 is a loop and I took the southerly loop about 50 miles out of my way. The southerly loop took me up and over Fort Mountain State Park. This was a narrow and curvy road, pretty, but not on my agenda.

Fort Mountain State Park, Georgia

Got as far as Blueridge and had to quit 75 miles shy of Highlands. I called Jodie and informed him that I would arrive tomorrow. This was OK as now I can now watch the last Survivor and CSI shows before Kathy. Stayed at a Days Inn for $60.00.

May 12, 2006 - Blueridge, GA to Highlands, NC 86 miles

Day broke partly cloudy but cold and I was only a short 86 miles from Highlands, but a long three-hour ride over to get there. After leaving Blueridge, GA I followed two bikers and we all stopped in Dillard, GA to gas up. They were from Phoenix, AZ and on their way to Myrtle Beach, FL. When they found out I was headed as far east as Cape Cod all they said was "Why?" At this time the whole northeast was under a major flood watch and the rain was still falling. I stopped for a sandwich in Dillard and after finishing found myself behind a fully loaded flat bed tractor-trailer hauling building stone up the hill to Highlands.   The road was too curvy to pass the truck so I just had to keep gearing down and follow that truck up the hill all the way to Highlands.

After arriving in Highlands, NC my cousin Jodie and his wife Caroline took me out to lunch at Fressers Courtyard Cafe. I had their local special, a Bacon Blue Cheese BLT that was wonderful. Afterwards, Caroline left us to run some errands. According to my cousin Jodie, Caroline is known around town as Highlands best "street walker" and when she is wearing her high heels she's elevated to the towns most "professional " street walker. In reality she is working with the local community (retail stores and various clubs) to solicit donations for the many community projects that Highlands supports.

While Caroline was working the good folks of Highlands Jodie drove me around the surrounding area pointing out the special locations and providing me with a better feel for the area. Highlands is a small but wealthy community with lots of history and a great deal of community activism. That evening both Jodie and Caroline had to work in the local Highlands Community Players theatre production of "I remember Mama." Caroline as stage manager and Jodie as production manager. They also both work in set construction. The play was very well done with a large production cast of over 33 people (including a cat) and 23 speaking parts.

Jodie is a busy member of the Rotary Club, Upper Cullasaja Water Shed Association, and tutors various students in the Literacy Program here in Highlands. Caroline is involved with the Garden Club, Tall Girls Club, Art

League, Highlands Community Fund, Chamber Music, Meals on Wheels and Holiday Meals Program and Shop with a Cop. They both operate businesses (Highland Chemical Corporation) and (Biocat Solutions Inc.)

This is why just about everyone in Highlands knows the Cooks!

Jodie and Caroline Cook in their Jaguar garage in Highlands, North Carolina

Jodie apparently has a soft spot for Jaguar cars as he owns seven along with a pickup truck and 4x4. Their house is new and very nice and built on a major cut out of the side of a mountain. Jodie doesn't drink but I purchased a very nice Chardonnay for Caroline. She drinks it like Kathy, over ice!

May 13, 2006   **Highlands, NC**   **Day off**

It was supposed to rain today but so far this morning, nothing! However, this morning's temperature was a brisk 37 degrees. Did a drive around in Jodie's XKE and visited "Bust your Butt Falls" on the Cullasaja (Sweet Water) River. Had lunch in town at Don Leons. Jodie is a very gracious man, a true "Southern Gentleman" but the graciousness stopped when I asked him if I could drive his XKE.

We mostly just sat around and talked about our families and it was good to reconnect after so many years. I sincerely hope sometime to meet my other cousins and their families. Jodies dad (my uncle and my dads younger brother) always lived on the east coast in the Atlanta area and our families had very little interaction. I guess the long distance apart was just too great.

May 14, 2006 - Highlands, NC to Mt. Airy, NC   266 miles

Rain delayed this morning's departure. Finally got underway about 9:30 AM. The roads were wet and it was spritzy most of the way to Asheville, NC. Getting into and out of Highlands took its toll on me. Lots of narrow and curvy roads combined with the cool temperature tired me out and I had to stop frequently to warm up and rest a bit.

I exasperated this fatigue even more by getting on the Blue Ridge Parkway (BRP). The BRP runs most of the way from Asheville to Virginia and it is a beautiful road. The speed limit is 45 mph and it has lots of viewpoint pullouts and magnificent vistas along its entire route. Great for motorcycles. The BRP climbed out of Asheville to the highest point in North Carolina (over 5000 feet). This morning it was stormy, cold, foggy and generally miserable. I had to get off on SR-80 and work my way back down into the valley where the elevation was lower and temperature warmer.

I got as far as Mt. Airy, NC, which is right on the border with Virginia, just ahead of a thunderstorm. Stayed at a Best Western ($59.00). I got unloaded and into the room just as the heavens opened up and I was once again under another tornado watch. After a while there was a lull in the storm and I could walk next door to the Truck Stop and get some dinner but no beer! They don't sell alcohol at truck stops. Bummer! Too tired, beat up and cold to go out looking for a source of beer so I just hunkered down for the night.

May 15, 2006 - Mt. Airy, NC to Middleburg, VA 312 miles

Day broke cloudy and cold. Had to stop twice to warm up. Hit a bit of rain on the last leg between I-66 and Middleburg.

Arrived at Frank and Mary-Ann's (Featherbed Lane Farm) about 3:00 PM a bit tired and wet. Frank hired me back in 1971 and was my first boss in the National Oceanic and Atmospheric Adminstration (NOAA). Between Frank and Mert Ingham (my second boss at NOAA) I was mentored well my first few years in the National Marine Fisheries Service and I owe my career to them both. Frank drove me around the farm. They now have 38 horses and a very cute new colt. Had a couple of cocktails with Frank while Mary-Ann made hamburgers and a salad. We watched the TV show 24 then I went to bed after taking a Benadryl.

Featherbed Lane Farm in Middleburg, Virginia

Day off to clean the bike. Frank took me to town to the local hardware store so I could buy a replacement seat bolt that had vibrated out of Ruby and was lost. I actually remember hearing it fall off the bike but didn't know, at the time, what it was. Stopped in town at the local watering hole for a couple of beers and talked a little business.

Returned to Featherbed Farm, fixed the bike, took some photos of the horses and checked my email. Frank gave me some training on his testosterone-laden sit down lawn mower. It took a bit of getting used to as I almost mowed Frank over as I trapped myself in the dreaded death spiral of mower uncontrollability. Even after almost putting him under his own mower he let me drive his John Deere tractor out over the fields and I was able to use the front scoop and shovel. Great fun and can only be topped with a little back hoe work at the L'Etoiles, still yet to be done.

Did a couple of Yahoo Map Quest plots and called Val (another work colleague and married to the second son of Kathy's and my oldest college friends) to delay my arrival by a day. Called the Silver Spring folks (Gary Soneira, Paul Chinn and Janet ? are old National Ocean Service work colleagues) and set up a lunch meet with them for tomorrow.

Called Vince and Marianne Zegowitz (dear friends and colleague). Vince and I had traveled the world together for many official meetings and I will stay with them on Thursday. Vince was supposed to be my travel companion for this trip but had to cancel in order to close on a beautiful home on Stony Creek overlooking the bay approaches to Baltimore. So far, except for a little cold I caught from Brucks all is going very well.

May 17, 2006 - Middleburg, VA to Alexandria, VA 88 miles

Rode into DC and tried to visit the US Marine Corps Iwo Jima Memorial but couldn't because of major construction and repairs going on. Looped it twice before giving up and headed for the Washington Cathedral (one of my most calming sites to visit) where exactly the same thing happened. It looks like they are building an underground Metro Station in the front yard of the Cathedral. What a mess and what a disappointment too.

Had lunch with Paul, Gary and Janet. Nice visit but not much has changed and it looks like they are all doing well enough. Gary presented me with a present of "Boudreaux's Butt Paste." Gary is very thoughtful that way.

Arrived at Val and Chris's place about 5:00 PM after fighting the DC traffic through town to Alexandria. It used to be so easy to get to Alexandria, but no longer. Val's sister, Kathy, was there visiting and helping out while Val winds down to "birthing" time. Chris was out of town and visiting his parents Tom and Sun Ji in Pagosa Springs, CO. Apparently, Sunji isn't doing so well with her Parkinsons. Val prepared a great dinner with lobster, scallops, asparagus served over pasta with a very nice New Zealand Riesling. After dinner we watched CNN and TWC while devouring pudding cups and (reduced fat) Klondike Bars. The evening's entertainment was watching her dog Guinness eating sprayed whipped cream out of mid air. What fun!

Kathy Growney (Val's sister on left) and Val Cannon in Alexandria, Virginia

May 18, 2006 - Alexandria, VA to Pasadena, MD 65 miles

Departed Chris and Val's late in the morning in a futile attempt to avoid the early DC rush hour traffic. Lots of road construction on the DC beltway with the associated ruts as well as trucks galore. Managed to avoid them and eventually found Vince and Marianne's new place in Pasadena, even though Vince gave me the wrong address and I stopped at his neighbors' place first.

Vince and Marianne really scored on a great place overlooking Stony Creek and out to Sparrows Point on the Baltimore outer harbor. I can see merchant ships cruising past the opening to Stony Creek. Great! Ran some errands with Vince while Marianne sold more houses. We drank some beers and grilled hamburgers. It was a great day with great friends.

View of Stony Creek from Vince and Marianne's back yard with the M/V Bony Boy tied up at their pier.

May 19, 2006 - Pasadena, MD   **Day off**

Woke up this morning with every intention of heading north; but alas, it was raining with another 40% chance tomorrow. TWC (The Weather

Channel) informs me of more thunderstorm activity in New England. That along with the early flooding may hold me over another day here.

Helped Vince with some of his "moving into a new house" jobs. Helped take down an old TV antenna, repair the roof with some very old and brittle shingles, cleaned out a couple of beer kegs, ran some more errands and moved furniture into the guest room where I will sleep tonight.

Met Bob and his wife Dottie, who are friends of Vince and Marianne's. Bob helped Vince bring the trawler M/V Bony Boy up from Florida. Bob also told me about the Harley Davidson factory in York, PA that I will be passing when again headed north. A "must" see. Vince had noticed a very small gas bleed from Ruby's petcock valve and I may be able to repair it in York. We'll see.

Had dinner at Vince and Marianne's son Mark and his wife Jen's new house along with Jen's parents Jack and Jackie. Vince spilled his wine at the dinner table. How refreshing that it wasn't me for a change. Mark and Jen have a real nice place and they are a very comfortable couple. They make you feel wanted and right at home.

Vince and Marianne Zegowitz in Pasadena, Maryland

May 20, 2006 - Pasadena, MD to Stamford, CN 329 miles

Departed Vince and Marianne's about 7:30 AM. Lots of clouds and a bit cool (at least on the motorcycle). Traffic was light and the roads good as I headed for York, PN. When almost to York I had to run a slalom course around five or six road kill deer carcasses scattered across the freeway. Apparently this bunch had wandered onto the interstate early that morning on a curve in the road and must all been hit by a semi, at the same time as they were scattered all over the road lanes and even the breakdown lane. What a mess!

Stopped in York, PA at Laugerman's Harley dealership to get Ruby serviced and fix the petcock bleed. Laugerman's took me in first as they usually do with cross-country riders and, while they were working on Ruby I had a chance to visit with other customers. Seems like most of their customers worked at the Harley factory and all suggested I should visit the Harley factory. Most of them were there to get their bikes inspected. Pennsylvania has a law that requires an annual inspection of all motorized vehicles. I also purchased a Laugerman's long sleeve shirt and Harley hat as I had lost my SD Padre hat when it blew out of my saddlebags somewhere in west Texas. You should always make sure that your saddlebags are fastened down before riding off.

The tech brought Ruby back to me after graciously filling up the fuel tank. To fix the petcock one has to remove the fuel tank and you have to drain the fuel tank before removing it. So, they refill it for you. It seems that the petcock on Ruby is an after market item and Laugerman's really didn't want to touch it. So the tech said he had to rebuild it. Now it bleeds even more! Should have left well enough alone I guess.

Stopped at the Harley factory on the way out of town but the only problem is they have no tours on Saturday. However the museum was open so I checked it out. We will have to stop again during normal working hours.

Even though I was first in line at Laugerman's it still took a few hours for them to service Ruby. If I hadn't stopped I could have very easily made it to Gail Ginnet's (an old Rhode Island friend) place in New Jersey but she wasn't home anyway so no loss. Gary Soneira had suggested I take this route (I-83 to I-81 to I-78 to I-287) which was a good choice even though it was all interstate roads. It was much more scenic and safer than the usual I-95 and New Jersey Turnpike. I stopped at a dump in Stanford, CN close to Westport and my old friend and NOAA colleague Lee Crist's gravesite.

May 21, 2006 - Stamford, CN to West Kingston, RI 180 miles

   Found Evergreen Historical Cemetery in Westport, CN but had to call Dar (Lee's widow) for directions as to which way to walk in order to find Lee's grave site. Good thing there was adequate cell phone coverage here as I was able to find "Our Beloved Lee" while talking with her. I sat down next to my old friend for a while and talked about the old times and Dar and apologized for not coming by sooner. I had forgotten that he was only 33 years old when he passed. Robert Wylie Crist was a loving husband, good friend, and was smart and curious. He was a good man and as "they" say, "the good die young." I guess that's why I'm still around.

Lee Crist's gravesite at Westport, Connecticut

I'd forgotten how long it takes to drive to Rhode Island from Westport Conn. even though I drove this route almost monthly for 13 years when I lived there. It took me almost three hours to get to Rhode Island. I did get off at Westerly and took US-1 (the coast road) up to SR-2 before cutting over to West Kingston and to friends Mary and Paul Arakelian's home. Mary and Kathy met a a La Leche meeting and being from southern California, we all hit it off well.

I was a bit early to Mary and Paul's, and because the weather was so good I continued on to Middlebridge. I saw a Buick parked in front of Gert Kavenaugh's place and took a chance and stopped. Gert was our secretary at the Atlantic Environmental Group many years ago and she had retired long before I left Rhode Island in 1984. On a whim and hopefully not scaring her to death, I rode into her yard. She was home and didn't even hear the Harley when I drove it in. She didn't recognize me at first but then remembered my voice and all was well. She fixed a pot of coffee and we chatted. She is now well into her 80's and still drinks, smokes and drives her car. She hasn't changed a bit in over 20 years. Go figure.

Gert Kavenaugh and me at Middlebridge, Rhode Island

Her husband Frank had passed away nine years earlier but Gert still hangs out with her sister and brother who live close by. Took a photo of us then headed on back to Mary and Paul's.

Paul prepared a great Chicken Ratatouille from the Silver Spoon Italian Cook Book we sent them as a previous Christmas gift. Genna, their daughter came for dinner too. She is such a pleasant young lady. Had a couple of exotic bourbon cocktails, a good dinner and Mary's homemade biscotti for dessert. Then I hit the wall.

May 22, 2006 - Rhode Island   Many days off

Paul's two longhaired German Shepards (that look like werewolves to me) Cleo and Maggie finally got used to me during the night. I left my door open so they could come in and check me out at their convenience anytime during the night. Sure enough, one at a time, they both paid me a visit. Mostly they came to my room to scratch themselves, probably spreading the dreaded deer tick Lyme disease to me as a welcoming present.

Cleo and Maggie, as usual, positioned between Paul and Mary and me

The next day Paul kept me company while I cleaned Ruby and was kind enough to move his car out of the garage and let me store Ruby inside. As usual, we discussed very personal issues. I came away with some good advice that Kathy and I need to come up with some "mutual activity" that we can both do together. Perhaps ballroom dancing?

May 23, 2006 - Rhode Island   Rest day

Took a day off to download a bit. Paul fixed a nice egg, muffin and sausage sandwich this morning and Mary made strong coffee to start the day. Mary had to work at her school and Paul had to prepare for his night school class tonight. However, Paul still took the time to drive me around through the old neighborhoods to get a feel for all the changes that have taken place here in South County. Paul even let me drive his vintage Porsche. I only ground 1st. gear twice completely forgetting how weak the synchromesh transmission feature was on a vehicle that old. No damage, just embarrassment.

After returning Paul showed me his building plans for the new house they are going to build on Othmar St. in Narragansett. He used a very simple Home and Garden house design software package that Genna (his daughter) bought him for Christmas. This software creates great floor plans, elevation plans and even three dimension views. I may have to buy similar software to design the house on our Nevada property (5@55). I tried playing with it a bit but the software wasn't very forgiving when designing a "round" house.

My stomach was a bit "rumbly" I think from the morning sausage and strong coffee. I drank some chocolate milk which usually works for me and took a nap around noon. I basically vegged out while Paul prepared for his class. By dinner time I was fine.

Mary and I cooked some extra chicken on the grill and mixed it with the previous night's leftovers for dinner. It was great!

In the early evening I was able to contact Bill and Johnnie Rodriguez who we met in our University of Rhode Island baby sitting cooperative. They invited me to a play they were reviewing "Waiting for Godot." I politely declined having "waited" for Godot once already in the past (He never showed up as I recall) and agreed to get together on Thursday. I also contacted another NOAA colleague Bob Benway and he was able to set up a lunch meeting also on Thursday at the Twin Willows with Jack Casey, Al Smelgelski and Robin Griswold (all old work colleagues and friends from my time in Narragansette." That should be fun sitting around with those old farts reliving the lies of the past. Also contacted Dar Crist and will try to see her tomorrow as well as try a drive by at the lab to see Jack Jossi and Grayson Wood (additional work colleagues). Next on the list are Dick and Bev Allen. Bev and Kathy had babies about the same time and we have been friends ever since. We all met in Lamaze class in 1975.

May 24, 2006 - Rhode Island   Just visiting

Mary and Paul's dogs and I are getting along better, but it is obvious that I am messing with their schedules, which is a perverse treat for me. They tolerate me but never let me between themselves and Mary and Paul's bedroom door when I'm walking around inside the house. They know their jobs and perform them well.

Rode up to Tower Hill where I can get some cell coverage. Missed Kathy again as she must have been at her physical therapy session. Contacted Dick Allen and set up a tentative meet after lunch as he is expecting to meet with his contractor some time today. Left another voice mail for Dar. Ran some errands to the drug store to pick up a spare set of earplugs and go to the post office to mail some post cards and my absentee ballot.

Met up with Dick Allen at the URI East Farm complex. He has gone back to school to earn a PhD. He and Bev are moving into a new condo in Westerly. No more mowing, trimming or painting for Dick. He is simplifying his life. Good for him.

Dick Allen at the University of Rhode Island East Farm in Narragansett, Rhode Island

Among other careers Dick used to be a commercial lobster fisherman when Kathy and I lived in Rhode Island. Dick and I partnered up on a scientific experiment where we would measure the inside body temperature of fish accidentally caught in his lobster traps and compare those temperatures with sea bottom temperatures; and try to correlate that data with the distribution of lobster. This experiment required that I go to sea on Dick's fishing boat for about three days and work as a crew member banding the keepable lobsters when they were pulled from the traps. It was on this trip that I realized there were three things that I would never do again in my life to earn money. One, buck hay, two logging, and the third was to fish commercially. All three require significant levels of physical work and are more suited for younger men. It was a surprise that the results from this experiment were published and I received many requests from folks all over the world for copies.

Dick's wife Bev was working at the Belmont Flower Shop that she now manages, so I rode over to surprise her. They both invited me to stay with them. They are such generous folks and always have been. They both looked in great shape and they are both very pleased grandparents.

Finally made contact with Dar and was invited for dinner with her and her daughters Cyd and Rych. I had to prepare the chicken because apparently none of them can cook. Either that or I was set up like Huck Finn. We had grilled chicken thighs seasoned with a rub that I made up from some miscellaneous old dried up spices I found buried in a back corner of Dar's kitchen cabinet. Mostly used paprika, chili powder, pepper flakes, salt and pepper and that seemed to work OK. Mashed red skin potatoes and fresh green beans topped it off. Dar's girls are now mature young women even at the tender age of 19. One attends George Washington and the other to Georgetown Universities in DC, and both are doing exceptionally well. Both are very mature, well educated and well adjusted and a pleasure to be around. Dar and Steve are "dating" again as time passes and trust increases. This is good news. Dar and I had some time to talk in private and reminisce a bit about our "Beloved Lee" and old times. Dar did yeoman's work taking care of Lee as he faced his own passing. He was a sweet heart of a man and I still miss him.

I was able to get back to the Mary and Paul's before dark, and in time for dessert.

With Dar, Cyd and Rych Detoy on their back deck in Wickford, Rhode Island

May 25, 2006 - Rhode Island   **Still visiting**

Today's plan is to visit Bill and Johnnie this morning and have a Twin Willows lunch with some of the old crew. Will have to make some calls too.

Paul and I compared Blood Pressures this morning. Paul thinks I should get another cardiologist. He doesn't know that I don't have a cardiologist just a regular GP that is good with animals.

Had a late breakfast with Johnnie and Bill. Took me two passes by their driveway to finally spot it and be able to turn into it. So much hedge overgrowth I was surprised Ruby made it through, let alone their car. No changes with Johnnie and Bill. They both looked good and still living in blissful harmony. I don't know how they do it and still stay as sane and as nice as they are. Sabrina, their daughter, and her husband, Stephan, have returned to Seattle and have a nice house in the Queen Ann section of town. I guess that is a desirable section of the city. I now have their new contact information. As expected, Johnnie says they would just love to see us. We fought off the caterpillars falling out of the trees and down my neck, the birds crapping on Johnnie and the cat scratching Bill. Oh, life goes on at the Rodriguez's and nothing changes very much. We discussed some Social Security issues (Bill wants to wait before collecting and Johnnie wants to start at 62, I believe Johnnie is correct, but Bill is stubborn). Took some photos, fought off the cats and left to pick up some birthday cards for old friends Nils and Grayson.

Visiting with Johnnie and Bill is always a very comfortable event. They are both so knowledgable and well read that I always learn something when talking with them. I'm proud to include them in my short list of real friends.

Breakfast with Johnny and Bill Rodriguez in their backyard in Peacedale, Rhode Island

Had the usual lunch at the Twin Willows (the dreaded Mert Burger). It is a large, grease dripping, heart attack of a burger that is absolutely a culinary treat. I guess some things never change or improve, but hell, why improve if you don't have to, eh? Bob Benway had managed to talk, old work colleagues, Jack Casey, Al Smigelski and Robin Griswold into attending. Funny, it had been so long since all of them had seen each other that it turned out to be more of a reunion for them. Even my best attempts to direct the conversation toward my motorcycle trip and me proved futile. No curiosity, or at best, no short-term memory curiosity prevailed among my old colleagues. I guess I should expect that my "test" is just that, "mine". Good thing I'm not a sensitive guy or would have dumped these friends a long time ago ;-).

Al had had a stroke but didn't show any visible signs of any problems. He told me he "steals from old ladies;" at least that's how he describes what he does for a living while retired. He actually is in the antique business and apparently VERY knowledgeable about it. Al is someone you would want on your side, but don't play poker with him. Sadly, Al has since passed since I first wrote this.

Jack still plays golf and bids his time between Rhode Island and Florida. No big fishing trips anymore. He looked real good but Dee Dee (his wife) has also passed since I first wrote this.

Bob still hunts for fun but works for his wife's traveling health care service and installs emergency monitor buttons in homes for shut Ins. In fact he just installed such a unit in Mert Ingham's old house in Wickford. He recognized it from the time we all helped Mert re-roof it.

Robin is still working at the lab and has two or three horses that keep her in the poor house. She will probably work until she dies. Talked about the old days and folks who had come and gone, the lab parties and fish frys. Robin was always a lot of fun at those lab Christmas parties! I gave Robin the birthday card I got for Grayson and asked her to put it on his desk for me.

It was good to catch up and see that my old friends hadn't changed so much after all. It was very nice of Bob to set this little luncheon for me. I can always depend on Bob.

Lunch with Al Smigelski, Bob Benway, Jack Casey and Robin Griswold on the deck of the Twin Willows in Narragansett, Rhode Island.

Tried to hook up with Greg Arakelian (Mary and Paul's son) by visiting his place of employment just to tell him how thoughtful I thought he was to send us that card about his Dad.   We talked a bit on the phone. Hopefully, we can all meet for dinner and Greg can give me the dirt on my son Colin when he visited him in San Francisco.

It was a great day for riding so I just rode many of the back roads from times past. I ended up at Watch Hill and had a bite to eat at the Olympia Tea

Room. The Olympia Tea Room is across the street from the old carrousel that Jet and Colin rode when they were little. Made contact with Lianne but not Jim Hannon. I'm getting a bit eager to get moving. Sunday will be my departure day from Rhode Island. Sent Kathy, Jet & Colin postcards.

May 26, 2006 - Rhode Island   Anxiously still visiting

Cleaned out Mary's hummingbird feeder and refilled it with sugar water. Also installed her bluebird bird house. Needed to borrow a step ladder from Paul to do this. I promised Mary I would do these chores before Paul and I went fishing.

Paul visited his bank and I the Post Office before heading off to URE Outdoor Store to purchase my non-resident fishing license. Paul generously insisted on buying my license. He said I was his guest. As usual I was doing my best to charm the proprietors of the store with my across-the-store humorous-banter with Paul, always in the second person when Paul stepped on one of my punch lines. I guess Paul doesn't think I'm as charming as I do. Damn, I always thought he did and that almost everyone else did too. Oh well, I'll have to work on this.

We fished the first dam on the Pacawtuck River near Wood River Junction. Paul fished the lake and I went downstream to fish the river. I managed to catch two small Brook trout and almost stepped on two very large black snakes that were sunning themselves on the trail. It's a sure sign of spring when the snakes are out warming themselves in the sun. Still a bit startling as they quickly move out of the way of your footpads. I didn't witness this but learned later that Paul had a misstep and tumbled down the trail and into the river. The aches and pains didn't show up until we were climbing the stairs at the Bon Vu Restaurant later that night.

We then drove further upstream to the area near the River Association Club House and another small dam. I used Paul's brand new waders and fished a beautiful section of that river just below the dam without even a bump. I was using Paul's spinning rod and reel but had tied on a very small nymph and was able with some practice to cast about 15 feet. Good enough to cover small stretches of the river and then I would wade up a bit and cast again. I was mid river when I made a cast and thought I saw a fish rise to it. To my surprise it wasn't a fish rising at all but rather a large Garter snake swimming across the river straight at me. At first I didn't realize it was a Garter snake and I was looking for a way to retreat and still look stylish while doing so when it swam up to me and then around me. That snake was swimming real fast. It pulled itself out on some low hanging branches in front of me to rest and set up an ambush position for small rodents. It was then I identified it as a Garter snake and what a nice specimen it was, well over an inch and half thick and about 3 ½ feet long and colorfully banded. I pointed it out to several other fishermen and kayakers and some of them were even able to spot it among the branches. One guy wanted to kill it but I manage to persuade him just to move along and fish somewhere else. One more wading movement upstream and I was able to land a very nice Rainbow. Photographed and released it.

In the mean time Paul was fishing upstream from me at the dam in the very fast water just below the dam and about six feet above the water from the concrete spillway. He was using an articulated Rapalla about four inches long with two sets of treble hooks. I would have bet $100 that a rig like that wouldn't catch trout but Paul said he has seen many come of that exact spot using that same type of rig. He informed me that he had already had a fish on and it broke his line! I no sooner voiced my concern over the lure he was using when he hooked up again. Well, I was certainly wrong. Paul caught the largest fish of the day. It was a very nice 1 lb. Rainbow trout. Wouldn't you know it, the fish swallowed that whole lure and was bleeding badly. This didn't matter at all to Paul because he is a meat eater and he was pissed that I had released my earlier fish. He was keeping his! Well, this was certainly a rush for both of us and we decided that enough fun had been had plus I was insisting on a beer. So off to the Wood River Junction Pub we went.

Paul Arakelian with the biggest fish of the day caught from the Wood River in Rhode Island

After returning home we measured our blood pressures again and mine was normal. Paul said it was either the calming effect of Rhode Island or the fishing. I told him it was the two Bass Ales at the Wood River Junction Pub. Then I took a nap. The next morning we ate that fish for breakfast.

That night, Mary, Paul, Greg, Genna and I went to the Bon Vu for dinner. It was so foggy you couldn't see past the outside deck. I had a chance to catch up with Greg and he told me of his visit out west to see a good friend of his in San Jose and he also hooked up with Colin. I now have the dirt with photo evidence to support it. Apparantly he doudn't close the deal on a young lady he had met. Before reaching the Bon Vu we stopped to see the local art exhibit at the Kingston Art Gallery. Greg had a photo on display there that won first prize. Good for him.

Mary wore a perfume that I really liked. It is called Hanae Mori.

Also reached Mert and Barbra and will see them either Sunday or Monday.

May 27, 2006 - Rhode Island   Last day

Basically this day was a staging day before my departure tomorrow. I have spent seven days here in Rhode Island and I'm eager to get underway. I still have farther east to travel before "officially" turning for home.

Did a last bit of laundry, played with Paul's design software, took some photos and made some calls.

Mary and Paul Arakelian at their home on Queens River Rd. in Rhode Island

That night we had dinner at Turtle Soup just down from the Coast Guard House. Greg brought his girl friend, Kathy, to meet us for drinks. She is very pretty and smart as whip. She was more than capable of putting up with my mindless banter. While Greg was there we called Colin to bust his chops. When Colin learned that I was drinking a Paul Arakelian 100 proof Manhattan he almost choked.

Beaver Tail, Conanicut Island, Rhode Island (Atlantic Ocean)

This was my last day in Rhode Island visiting old and "close" friends plus visiting all the old special places that are still locked in my minds eye. Rhode Island is where both Jet and Colin were born and Kathy and I made many close friends here. After almost a week in one place I was anxious to get moving as I still had further east to travel before turning for home

May 28, 2006 - West Kingston, RI to South Denis, MA   141 miles

Departed West Kingston about 7:00 AM with good weather in the forecast. Stopped in New Bedford. MA for gas. A fellow from Mumbai, India operated the gas station and most of his customers had their names and prison ID numbers tattooed on the backs of their necks. They all seemed to like Ruby and were "very" complimentary about how nice she looked. Some even called their friends to come take a look at it.

I had a good cell phone signal here and was busy taking care of some voicemail messages and checking in with people. This provided ample time for my newly discovered BFF prison friends to call their buddies for a drive by "look-see". This was making me a bit anxious so I decided to get underway right there and then.

Rode up SR-6 along the coast and stopped at Jim Hannon's (another old work colleague) place in Wareham, MA even though I was never able to reach him on the phone. You see Jim is the reason I was on this trip. About 17 years earlier Jim turned me on to an article in Esquire magazine that had a piece in it about "The 50 things every man has to do." One of those 50 things was to ride a Harley across the United States. Even back then, with no motorcycle experience under my belt, I thought this was something I could do. After all you can't easily ride a horse across the country any more, like Kit Carson did. (Actually, Kit Carson rode a mule most of his life). Jim wasn't there so I settled on taking a picture of Ruby and me in front of his magnificent house and then headed east to Mert and Barbara Ingham's. Found out later that Jim was on vacation and out of the state and didn't get any of my telephone messages until he returned home long after I had passed through.

My visit with Mert and Barbara was very nice. Mert was my supervisor and mentor for many years while I was working in Rhode Island. Barbara insisted that I stay the night. I don't think they get much company and they wanted some. She had planned a sausage, chicken and pork cacciatore which sealed the deal. Mert and I discussed old times and had some laughs and I went to bed at my usual time but not until I finished Barbara's Lemon Ice dessert. I was teasing Mert about all the editing he used to do with our research papers and told him that I would send him this journal to edit before releasing to the general public. NOT! You see Mert has published some memoirs in the past and I've always told him he doesn't have enough sex, drugs or rock and roll in any of his work and I want to show him how to "spice" up a manuscript a bit.

Our visit was very comfortable. The last thing Mert said to me before leaving this morning was, "Tell Lianne (another dear work colleague) hello for me and tell her that she and you were the most productive members of AEG." I told him we already knew that but thanked him anyway. Coming from Mert that is the equivalent of a long tongue kiss. I may have to slack off on my teasing him a bit.

Sadly, Barbara is another one of those I visited on this trip that has past away since writing this. She was a wonderful person and one of the nicest I've ever encountered.

Dinner with Mert and Barbara Ingham at their home in South Denis, MA

May 29, 2006 - South Denis, MA to Westfield, MA 193 miles

Departed Mert and Barbara's place about 7:30 AM trying not to awaken their neighbors with the sound of Ruby. **(I'M FINALLY HEADED WEST AND HOME).** Barbara was up before me. She had the lights on, candles lit and the coffee made. She was a real sweetheart hostess who made you feel so very much welcomed. I really hope I didn't put her out too much.

Stopped to visit Lianne and her partner Peter. I teased her about making me a large breakfast and she took the bait. Bacon, eggs, toast, coffee and juice. Who knew she was so domesticated? Peter seems to be a very nice man and Lianne is happy. So that is good enough for me. I was sorry to have missed Haley as she was at an NRA retreat recreating living conditions during colonial times with accurate costumes and cooking et.al. I bet she hates it, but will have to wait and see. Lianne said she really wanted a ride on a Harley. Lianne said that I would be the only one she would trust to give her that ride. That was nice.

Breakfast with Lianne Dunn and Peter on their back deck in Sandwich, MA

Unfortunately, Peter too, has recently passed away since I started writing this. Peter was a very gracious and a wonderful family man. He was very good to Lianne and he will be missed by many.

Departed Lianne's and Peter's place about 10:30 and took my time riding west to Westfield, MA. Just enjoying the good weather and basking in the knowledge that I was finally headed west and home.

Arrived at Chris and Kim Juden's (my oldest friend's son) about 4:00 PM but no one was home. I had tried calling earlier but no answer on their cell phone. I figured they were celebrating May Day with friends and were out of cell range. So I went looking for AC and beer as it was a bit hot and humid and when I returned they were just arriving back from a weekend adventure into the Finger Lakes region of upper New York State with some friends. They scored a case of wine, a mixture of varietals from ice wine to Riesling & Chardonnay with a few reds.

Kim put together a real nice dinner on very short notice. She prepared steak, green beans, salad, rice, wine and dessert. Kim knows her way around a kitchen. Everything was just fine especially when you consider my early arrival probably contributed to the stress level.

Little Gabriella (Elle) was a trooper even after having traveled in a car for five hours before returning home. She sure is cute and smart. The dogs (Kaya and Colby) are a big part of their little family and they seemed to accept me as a "friendly". Had to remove a tick from one of them. As the weather warms the ticks get thicker.

Chris and Kim have really fixed up this ranch style home from what it was before they bought it. Before it was very dark. New light paint and tile as well as kitchen fixtures have gone a long way in improving the looks of the place.

Chris is a Physicians Assistant and in demand everywhere. He works at two different doctors offices and the Emergency Room at the local hospital. Kathy and I have always been very proud of Chris and the way he conducts himself in life.

Chris downloaded all 185 of my photos from my camera and burned a CD that he will mail home for me. Recharged the camera battery and now have a fresh pallet with which to continue the trip. They did a load of laundry for me so I'm really ready to head west now.

Chris and Kim Juden with little Gabriella in Westfield, Massachusetts

May 30, 2006 - Westfield, MA to Northfield, MA 67 miles

Not in a big hurry this morning as I didn't have far to go. I rode up SR-10 to 47 to 63 that runs along side of the Connecticut River. Passed through several old historic towns. What a nice ride. Just before arriving in Northfield a red tail hawk crossed in front of me about windshield height and no more than 10 feet in front of Ruby. What a sight. It was absolutely beautiful.

Arrived at 4 Star Farm at 12:30 PM but Bonnie and Gene (old friends from when Kathy and I lived in Rhode Island) were still occupied elsewhere so I waited on the front porch of their new home. What a place! Turned out they were waiting for me down at the farm office and Bonnie came up to the house to get me. She let me in, I stowed my gear and we drove back down to the office. Bonnie had some errands to run so I waited for Gene to arrive. He was dealing with an irrigation issue. When we hooked up I rode around with him as he showed me the improvements they had made to the farm as well as keeping track of the irrigation problem.

Bonnie and Gene L'Etoile on the deck of their spectacular home in Northfield, MA

They are starting a new project with their son Nathan to raise Bass fish for stocking into private fishing preserves. They are still building the ponds just behind the house. Sounds exciting and apparently Nathan has done considerable research on how to do this for profit.

Had a nice visit and Bonnie begged off from having to attend a Selectman Meeting in town so we could hang out. Had a great dinner and reminisced a lot about the old days. However, there was no time for me to play with any heavy equipment because I was eager to get headed west.

Bonnie and Gene are always the most gracious of hosts and I always feel comfortable around them. They are indeed great friends.

May 31, 2006 - Northfield, MA to Canandaigua, NY 328 miles

       Got an early start under cool but clear weather. Followed the Mohawk Trail across Massachusetts to New York. The Mohawk Trail basically follows the Deerfield River, Cold River and Green River across the top of Massachusetts, all very nice looking trout streams. There was lots of pretty country and fishable water along this route. Stopped for gas in North Adams. The gas station attendant and I talked fishing for a while. He even gave me a map of Vermont to use in three years when Kathy and I make this trip. At the direction of the gas station attendant I jumped south here at North Adams, MA to meet up with US-20 and followed that all the way across New York.

Along the beautiful Mohawk Trail in upper Massachusetts

Riding along US 20 I unknowingly passed by the Cooperstown, NY turnoff. After I had returned home and Jet and I realized I was within 12 miles of Cooperstown and didn't stop, he was absolutely dumbfounded that I didn't visit the Baseball Hall of Fame. Actually, I was too. It just wasn't on my radar screen by that time into the trip.

Later this morning I was following a dump truck when I noticed oncoming traffic slowing to a stop. All of a sudden the dump truck locks up his breaks to avoid hitting a very nice doe that had jumped onto the highway.

I was glad the dump truck was between the deer and me. By the way, New York has some BIG deer.

The roads were a bit rough and poorly marked in Albany, NY but for most of this ride the trip was very good and with relatively light truck traffic.

Noticed several newish trucks parked along side the highway displaying "For Sale" signs. I wonder if this is a measure of the health of our economy? So many new trucks and perhaps folks not being able to make the payments?

Stopped for gas this afternoon and when I turned Ruby off I heard a loud "pop" sound that sounded like a light bulb being dropped on a garage floor. The sound seemed to come from the other side of the parking lot next to me but I didn't notice anything out of the ordinary. I stayed at such a nondescript motel in Canandaigua that I didn't even record the name in my journal.

June 1, 2006 - Canandaigua, NY to Welland, Canada 140 miles

Departed the nondescript motel around 9:00 AM under threatening skies and continued west on US-20. Contacted Ron Fordyce (another work colleague who traveled the world with me in past years) and he suggested filling up the gas tank on the US side as it is less expensive here than in Canada. I did, at a Sunoco station and asked what highway to take to get to the Fort Erie Bridge. I was given instructions to I-90 (the NY Thruway that goes to Erie). It then started to rain (the earlier threat was realized) and I soon realized that I-90 was incorrect. I got off at the first opportunity (it cost me $0.15) and the tollbooth guy gave me the correct instructions to get to the "Peace Bridge." Seems the Canadians call it the "Fort Erie Bridge" and the Americans call it the "Peace Bridge." Being on the American side where we make our own signs, all I saw were signs to the "Peace Bridge."

About this time the truck traffic in the Buffalo area really picked and so did the rain. Two different truck drivers at two different stoplights told me that my headlight was out. I then remembered on the previous day when I stopped in Canandaigua and turned off the bike that I heard a sound like someone had dropped a light bulb across the parking lot from where I stopped. I guess that was when my headlight gave up. I didn't realize the light had blown because the brights still worked. Eventually, even the brights gave up.

I arrived at Ron and Sherri's at about 1:00 PM. They told me there was a custom Harley shop (Extreme Choppers) nearby that could help me. I called and made an appointment right then. I unloaded by gear and Ron and Sherri gave me a bucket of soapy water and a hose to clean the bike. I wanted to get most of the road grime off the bike before taking it into the shop. Rain and crappy roads can really dirty up a bike quickly. I followed Ron over to Extreme Choppers where they took it in and said it would be finished by 5:00 PM closing time. I had them repair the headlamp, replace the seat bolt that had vibrated out (again) and change the oil. They did a good job, and the price of labor there is about half of what it is here in the US.

Breakfast with Ron and Sherri Fordyce in Welland, Ontario, Canada

Ron drove me around Welland and the neighboring towns along the famous Welland Canal. The Welland Canal has been in existence for over 150 years and bypasses Niagara Falls, so ship traffic can get into and out of Lake Erie and the Great Lakes via the Niagara River. Didn't have time to visit Niagara Falls so will save that for the next trip.

We then went back to Extreme Choppers to pick up Ruby. The techs hadn't finished when we arrived so we just hung out and waited. While waiting, a rather "over the top" or I should say almost out of her top woman showed up. She was a friend to most of the guys there at Extreme. She was rather buxomy and very vivacious and loved to be the center of attention. I know she got Ron's and mine.

That evening Sherri prepared a great dinner (actually one that I had been promised for years now) of moose steak and venison sausage along with potatoes, broccoli and carrots all topped off with a fine Niagara Red wine followed by dessert. We reminisced about past adventures in foreign countries with mutual friends and in general just caught up on family news. Both Ron and Sherri thought the moose meat would be "gamey" but I thought it was just fine and had a second steak just to make sure. Finally after all these years of Ron talking about his freezer being full of moose meat, I got a taste. Ron and Sherri have both a hunting camp and a cottage located north of them in the Georgia Bay region of Ontario and they invited (or maybe I coerced an invitation) Kathy and me for a trip up there in three years when Kathy retires. Ron said there are Lake Trout in his lake and I saw the photos, so we're there for sure

June 2, 2006 - Welland, Canada to Battle Creek, MI 364 miles

Departed Welland under cloudy skies and followed Highway 3 to London, Ontario when I jumped up on Highway 402 to cross back into the US at Port Huron. This route allowed me to miss the heavy traffic and scenic city of Detroit. Damn, maybe next time. As in New York, I also noticed many cars (not trucks this time) parked along the side of the road sporting "For Sale" signs. I guess Canadians don't need trucks as much as we Americans do.

Ah, Spring in southern Ontario, Canada. The winter wheat is approximately a foot high with about two months to go before harvesting. The flowers are blooming, the trees are leafing and the birds are breeding. In fact they are so fervent in their breeding that some don't even take notice of a speeding Harley passing under them as they go through their spectacular "love dives."

A female (I can only assume) during one of those "love dives" and trying to avoid pursuit by an amorous male, managed to avoid my windshield, pass under my right arm and up over my right shoulder leaving only a small feather stuck to my right handlebar.   The male managed to turn away from my right shoulder at the last possible second avoiding a collision and certain death, not to mention the possible heart attack to me! All of this happened in just a nanosecond and I was helpless to do anything in the way of avoiding this possible catastrophe.

There were no apparent causalities from this event, but I imagine the female had to stop and rest just to catch her breath after just barely avoiding a gruesome death impacting either Ruby or myself. I figure the male probably took advantage of her shortness of breath to consummate his pursuit. In the end I was just thankful that they both were small sparrows and not red tail hawks like the one I saw earlier in Northfield, MA.

Aside from this love bird event the ride was uneventful. Just pretty farm land and Quakers or Amish folks using horses for their buggies and wagons as they rode along the same rode as me. Saw many farms that had abandoned drying sheds boarded up on their properties. It turns out that these were tobacco drying sheds. In the old days Ontario used to be a tobacco growing area. Who knew? I always associated tobacco with the southern US.

After crossing back into the US I took I-69W to I-94W through Lansing, MI toward Battle Creek, MI. I was trying to make Kalamazoo because who wouldn't want to stay in a town name Kalamazoo? Thought I was good to go as I was riding into "blue sky". However, upon turning west onto I-94 I rode directly into a thunderstorm and it quickly forced me off into the city of Battle Creek. On the positive side, I like corn flakes just fine. I exited one off ramp too soon and had to ride around a bit before I found the appropriate dirt bag motel. Again, I didn't record or remember the name, so not rating stars from me.

My eyes were a bit itchy for a second day in a row so I went to bed with a Benadryl.

June 3, 2006 - Battle Creek, MI to Eau Claire, WI 490 miles

Departed Battle Creek about 8:00 AM under fairly clear skies. Mostly sunny with low cumulus clouds all day. Roads were clear and good until the Loop in Chicago. Never seen so much construction, bad roads, detours and closed off and on ramps. Tried to locate an old friend (Elaine O'Sullivan) but was unsuccessful. (Note: Elaine used to be Tim, and my best childhood friend from Junior and Senior High School that help me get into competitive gymnastics, surfing and was Best Man at my wedding). To this day I still miss her and wish she had reached out to me within the bounds of her new identity.

Gained a time zone today and with good roads leaving Chicago, no wind and little traffic I was able to make it all the way to Eau Claire, Wisconsin.

I called my Aunt and Uncle, Theda and Al Slagle, and Al told me that he and Theda go to bed about 6:00 PM and sleep late and that they are not the same people I last visited. I assured him that I would stay at a motel so as not to bother them. Al was very frank and pleased with this idea. I will try and contact my cousins Lanny and Scott when I get there.

I don't plan to stay too long.

June 4, 2006 - Eau Claire, WI to Park Rapids, MN 290 miles

Departed Eau Claire about 7:30 AM under clear skies. Lots of road kill deer along I-94. The Wisconsin Dept. of Highways must have a carcass patrol that goes out every morning to pick up the casualties. Saw many fresh traces of kills (smudges of animal fat and blood) but no carcasses? I doubt if they crawled away by themselves.

Arrived Park Rapids about 1:00 PM and was able to visit with Al and Theda for a little while. We agreed that I would bring back some dinner later and I left to find a motel. It turned out that my cousin Scott worked at the Ace Hardware store just across the street from Theda and Al's so I stopped by to say hi before heading off to find a motel. I recognized Scott but of course he wouldn't know me as I came on him so unexpectedly. We talked briefly and agreed to meet later at Theda and Al's after he got off work.

Got a room at the C'mon Inn and contacted my other cousin Lanny (Scott's brother) Jones and he agreed to come pick me up tonight after Al & Theda retired. Went to the local grocery store and picked up some already prepared chicken, three bean salad and twice baked potato for dinner. Went back to Theda and Al's for dinner and did a load of laundry. I ended up leaving my old denim shirt that I had worn this entire trip in their basement. It was pretty threadbare but I hate giving up on a garment of clothing that still has some life left to it.

Al and Theda (Huddleston) Slagle in their kitchen in Park Rapids, MN

We had as good a visit as could be expected I guess. Al is still OK but he is aging fast and Theda is pretty much mired in her dementia. I couldn't be positive that she even knew who I was. I had to show her my Drivers License to prove to her that I was Glenn Cook's son. Theda remembered Glenn but not her sister (my mother) Alberta. She referred to Glenn as a "good lover." I wonder from where that came?

Sadly, both my Aunt Theda and Uncle Al have passed away since I started writing this piece. Thankfully, in earlier years I did have the opportunity to interview Theda and capture on tape stories about her and my mother's earlier life and being born in a sod house on the Oklahoma pan handle.

Later Scott came by my motel and we had a chance to reacquaint a bit more than we could at either the store or at Al & Theda's place. Turns out that Scott has a Honda Gull Wing motorcycle. Next time I'll give him more of a "heads up" that I'm coming and maybe we can go for a ride together.

Lanny picked me up at the motel and took me out to his and his wife, Sandy's place on the lake. We all had a nice visit and caught up on family stories and genealogical information. Lanny returned me to my motel fairly early.

My cousins Lanny and Scott Jones at my motel in Park Rapids, MN

After Lanny dropped me off at the C'mon Inn I decided to do a little exploring around Park Rapids. After all, I was leaving tomorrow, it was a Sunday night and I really hadn't had any free time to learn about this town. As expected, I did stumble into a local dive bar. These are my usual favorite places to get a feel for townsfolk, politics, and sports and in general just what's happening in the community. There was also a Minnesota Twins baseball game on the TV. It being a Sunday night I wasn't surprised that there were only three other folks in the bar and it was obvious to me they had been there a while. Two young men and one rather "plumpish" young lady, who must have liked the sound of her voice as she was loud and quite the talker, were sitting at the bar drinking beer. Time to kick back, order a beer, watch a little baseball and listen to the folks at the bar.

It was difficult to avoid overhearing their conversation even when trying to watch a ballgame from the other side of the room. The young lady was a bit coarse and rough around the edges in her conversation with her two friends. The gist of their talk concerned just how long one of the young men would have to wait before receiving his turn for oral sex promised earlier. Apparently, the other young man had already been serviced and his buddy was getting impatient for his turn. The lady friend kept stalling trying to coerce one more beer from the two men before honoring her earlier commitment. I guess the second trick was getting low on expendable cash and had to borrow a couple of dollars from his friend to buy the aforementioned libation for the young lady.

About this time there was a strong hit by a Minnesota Twins player and my attention was re-directed to the TV. After the several instant replays I heard the front door of the bar open and the two youngsters returned to their barstools. I guess the obligation had been fulfilled out in the parking lot during the instant replays.

Returned to my motel, wrote some post cards. Tomorrow I head for the Dakota's and open prairie.

June 5, 2006 - Park Rapids, MN to Selby SD   364 miles

Departed Park Rapids at 8:15 AM and dropped off my post cards at the post office and rode into a mild weather system I knew was coming my way from Fargo, ND.

I hit rain squalls twice just east of Bismarck, ND before breaking through to the warm side and blue skies with fluffy white clouds. I turned south on US-83 and will be on this same highway all the way to Paradise, Kansas before I turn west again.

Lots of flat up here along this US-83.

Picked up a tail wind and all was going good until I had to detour onto a dirt road for 15 miles as I passed from North Dakota into South Dakota. Saw lots of Prairie Dog colonies today. Those critters can really tear up a lot of hillside with their multiple interconnected tunnels.

Made it as far as Selby, SD and stayed at the Selby Motel for $47.00. I headed downtown (about 2 blocks away) and found the local watering hole. Met some of the locals, all of whom were very nice and supportive of an old biker on a long road trip. They provided me with some of the history of the area. The bartender was the father of the son who really owned the place but as the father was on the Town Council and had to attend a meeting, his wife came in to mind the bar. Ordered a hamburger and fries for din din.

Called Kathy.

Thought for the day: It's the bugs coming straight at you that you can't see that hurt the most. Today I took two hits in exactly the same spot over my left eye that felt like I was shot with a 22-caliber pistol each time. The first hit really got my attention, but the second hit in "exactly" the same spot forced me to stop and check the bleeding.

June 6, 2006 - Selby, SD to Oakley, KS   511 miles

D-Day anniversary!

Departed at 7:30 AM under clear skies, cool temperatures and an open road in front of me. During the first hour I passed two farm vehicles and 2 pick up trucks all going in the opposite direction. Nothing behind me except empty road.

Lots of flat up here along this US-83.

Along US-83 somewhere in either South Dakota or Nebraska (not much difference)

I understand why our early settlers with an ilk toward farming would settle in this region. Good dirt that was easy to plow. Just passed a "Watch for Deer" sign a while ago. If there are deer out here they must live underground like the Japanese soldiers on Iwo Jima. There is nothing growing more than six inches high over 360 degrees of horizon. Oh, wait, there is a clump of trees way the hell over there to my right. Maybe the deer hide out there! Sure enough, a couple of miles later I spot two deer off to my left silhouetted by the morning sun. They were too far away for me to be able to see any dirt on them from climbing out of their burrows.

Not too many fences up this way. I guess there is no need to fence wheat, soybeans or corn. Oh, I suppose, occasionally some will make a break for the other side of the road but they're mostly sedentary and well controlled by the farmers.

About this time I thought I saw a plump road runner crossing the road in front of me, but then thought it might have been a wild turkey hen. Then Ruby flushed two more that flew across the road in front of me and they turned out to be ring neck pheasants. Saw many more this morning and wondered with all the open space around here why they chose to live so close to the highway?

Lots of flat up here along US-83.

Passed two prairie dog communities along the way today. One ran across the road in front of me. They look odd running on asphalt.

Spring has been good up here. Passed several new calves and foals among the many herds of cattle and horses I passed.

Passed a sign near Pierre, SD that read, "movie Dances with Wolves was filmed nearby."

Made it all the way to Oakley, Kansas and stayed at the Annie Oakley Motel for $36.00. Walked into town (two blocks again) and ate at Buffalo Bills. Had some tacos and beers. The tacos were touted as the "special" but Oakley is a long way from Mexico!

Horses near the Standing Rock Indian Reservation in SD

June 7, 2006 - Oakley, KS to Alamosa, CO   291 miles

Got an early start at 6:30 AM under partly cloudy skies and a moderate temperature. Had hopes of making it to Pagosa Springs today.

Still lots of flat out here along "scenic" US-83.

Kansas has plenty of cattle feedlots scattered along US-83 and are easily identified even if out of sight and miles away by their very distinct smell. Makes one thankful for allergies and favorable wind conditions.

Finally turned west toward the Rocky Mountains today on US-50 but it still took two hours of riding before they came into sight. I stopped in Lamar, Colorado for a late breakfast.

Continued on US-50 west to La Junta where I caught SR-10 that runs up to Walsenburg. SR-10 is one of the bleakest roads I've been on so far. Absolutely nothing out here and I don't know how anything could survive. I saw one dead horse leaning up against a barbed wire fence. Probably died of thirst or boredom. Also saw a pronghorn antelope standing with his front legs on the road and his hind legs on the shoulder just watching me as I rode by. I was by him so fast that if he had spooked I wouldn't have been able to avoid him for sure.

Gained another time zone today but the wind buffeting was fatiguing and when an afternoon thunderstorm blew up I gave it up and stopped in Alamosa. So, no Pagosa Springs today. Called Tom and Sun Ji (dear friends from my college days) and told them that I would see them tomorrow.

Found a shoe repair shop in town and purchased replacement inner cushion soles for my boots. I'll have to have these motorcycle boots resurrected when I return home.

Wrote and mailed some post cards to those interested in this little adventure. Should make it to Pagosa Springs tomorrow.

June 8, 2006 - Alamosa, CO to Pagosa Springs, CO   92 miles

Departed Alamosa about 7:30 under cloudy and cool conditions. Stopped in Del Norte for breakfast. I was in no particular hurry as Tom and Sun Ji wouldn't be there when I arrived anyway. Sunj had a doctor's appointment in Durango that would prevent them from getting home until early that afternoon.

Basically followed the Rio Grande River up the San Luis Valley to South Fork. Very nice country and it reminds me a lot of our five acres in the Pinenut Mountains. Climbed up and over Wolf Creek Pass. At 10,900 feet it was plenty cold and there was still snow in the North facing crevices on the mountain. Stopped at an overlook viewpoint and took some photos of the Pagosa Springs Valley and the headwaters of the San Juan River which runs west into Lake Powell.

Overlook just outside Pagosa Springs, Colorado

Arrived at Tom and Sunj's place about 10:30 AM. They had left a key for me under the mat along with a note that they would return around noon. I quickly made myself at home. Unloaded Ruby, did my laundry and washed Ruby. She really needed it. I finished and covered her up just as a rain squall blew up and passed over.

I grabbed a beer out of the reefer and sat on the front porch watching the rain and lightening play across the valley and mountains. Very relaxing and soothing to me to watch "Mother Nature" like this. I felt so comfortable that it made a believer out of me just to be sitting there. I've always felt that everybody should believe in something. I know I do, now I believe I'll have another of Tom and Sunji's beers!

Tom and Sunj arrived home about 1:00 PM and they had fought rain both going to and coming from Durango. After settling in and getting organized we all went out for a late lunch at the Hogs Breath Inn. Tom had to lend me a shirt as mine were still in the dryer. As I mentioned before I had left my "road" shirt in Theda and Al's basement and my good (going out to lunch or dinner) shirt was in the dryer.

Returned from lunch and Sunj took a nap. Her medication for the Parkinson's disease really knocks her out. Tom and I talked and played with Kato. Kato is a female Hound and Ridgeback mix that Tom thought was a male. After learning from Val that Kato was female made no difference to Tom, Kato remains a "he". In Tom's defense his eyes aren't what they used to be.

Tom and I sat on the front porch and watched the rain and lightening that was continuing to play over the valley and on the mountains. Very nice!

June 9, 2006　　　　　**Pagosa Springs, CO**　　　　　**Rest day**

Took a day off for some R&R. Kathy departs today for her library meeting in Baltimore. I was supposed to call her for a wake up call at 3:30 AM west coast time, but screwed up the time zone thing and called her at 2:30 AM instead. At least she won't miss her plane.

Out for breakfast at Victoria's Parlor then did a drive around Pagosa Springs and the surrounding environs. Saw some really beautiful country and some very large and expensive homes. Went shopping as Sunj is determined to prepare Momma Cannon's Pork Chops. Tom doesn't cook and Sunj is becoming too debilitated to cook much anymore so they eat out often if not always. So, making Momma Cannon's Pork Chops will require a bit of assistance from me. No problem, I'll just do what Sunj tells me to do and keep the wine glasses full.

Good friends of Tom and Sunj, Tom and Ming Steen, came over for dinner. Seven years ago their son Shawn was at our house for dinner. He was attending a summer seminar internship at a company in La Jolla. He is now a doctor in Dallas, Texas. His sister Courtney is doing the same internship and Kathy and I will have her over for dinner too. I guess Courtney is not only a great student but also good with horses. She is helping to train horses at her temporary home in Valley Center, CA.

Tom and Ming are very enthusiastic cyclists. They are training for a five day, 400 mile, 39,000 foot elevation changes (over five mountain passes) camping trip along with about 3000 other cyclists. Of course there is not an once of fat on either one of them. They were also kind enough to invite Nils (my ski buddy) and myself to stay with them if we ever decide to ski Wolf Creek. Just may take them up on their generous offer.

Tom and Sun Ji Cannon's living room in Pagosa Springs, Colorado

After folks left, Sunj went to bed and Tom and I took care of the dishes. Tom and I had a Scotch and discussed worldly and personal issues until we both felt properly vented and fatigued. I always appreciate these conversations because Tom is very knowledgeable about world history and continually points out parallels between current and past times. We are doomed to repeat our mistakes unless we have world leaders that are also students of history. Unfortunately Sun Ji has since passed away and is sadly missed by many of us.

Tomorrow I head for Monument Valley. I have known of it, flown over it, and seen it in dozens of movies and calendars. Now I will get to see it for myself, and better still, ride Ruby through it. Finally!

June 10, 2006 - Pagosa Spring, CO to Flagstaff, AZ 419 miles

Departed Tom and Sun Ji's at 8:00 AM under clear skies and cool temperatures.

Stopped in Cortez, Colorado for gas and to call Kathy and Jet. Both sounded well and Kathy was about to go on the Zegowitz's trawler M/V Boney Boy for a little cruise on Baltimore's inner and outer harbor, just three weeks after I did the same thing with them.

Had to make the obligatory stop at Four Corners (where the States of Arizona, Utah, Colorado and New Mexico meet). This location was mapped and surveyed in the 1860s but recent GPS results indicate that this position is in error by 2.5 miles. Still, pretty good survey work for the 1860s. It is mostly a Navaho Indian tourist trap. Most of today was spent traveling through the Navaho Indian Reservation. Made the Monument Valley loop via Bluff, Mexican Hat and Goulding's. Crossed over the San Juan River (that originates in Pagosa Springs) near Mexican Hat just before it meets Lake Powell. Absolutely "stunning" geological formations and would love to take some time to wander around in the fall and winter months.

Monument Valley on US-163 between Mexican Hat and Gouldings, UT

Lots of wind today but managed to make it to Flagstaff, Arizona. Had to push hard to get off the Navaho Indian Reservation lands in order to be able to get a beer at happy hour. Saw herds of sheep, goats and some species of small scrawny cattle today. Plenty of open range and most were right along side of the road.

Stayed in a dirt bag hotel next to the railroad tracks in the old part of town. Either a Russian or Croat operated it, I wasn't sure. I couldn't even open the door to the first room he gave me. The key wouldn't work. So he gave me another. Thanks! The shower floor still had the hair from the previous occupant or occupants.

If all goes well I may make it home tomorrow. YEA!

June 11, 2006 - Flagstaff, AZ to Cardiff, CA   494 miles

Departed Flagstaff at 6:00 AM. Very cold beginning, but as I descended into the lower desert things warmed up a lot. By the time I got down to the Colorado River at Needles the temperature was well over 100 degrees. I could smell the finish line now and even though today was going to be a long hard pull I still felt the need to get home!

Followed I-40 to SR-95 south at Needles. Followed SR-95 to Vidal Junction and cut over to meet I-10, then took the Mecca cutoff to pass by the northern end of the Salton Sea. I then took the Borrego Springs Road up and over the mountains. I stopped at the Hideout Bar for a beer and coincidently met up with Doug (the owner of the Kraken where I started this trip). Doug bought me a beer.

Arrived home about 3:30 PM. Cleaned up and went down to the Kraken to listen to some Blues and drink a few Bass Ales and celebrate my successful trip. Jet came over 5:00 and we got caught up on all the recent news.

I was glad to be home even though it seemed a bit anticlimactic. It was as if I didn't want it to end. I knew tomorrow it would be an odd feeling not to be climbing aboard Ruby and just riding somewhere. I was happy that I had done this trip on my own terms even though it was a physical as well as psychological challenge. I guess many people have done such a trip but "most" of us have not. In hindsight, I would do this again in a heartbeat. It was a wonderful adventure.

Like the lyrics in the song "It's my Life" by Bon Jovi say:

- It's my life
- It's now or never
- I ain't gonna live forever
- I just want to live while I'm alive

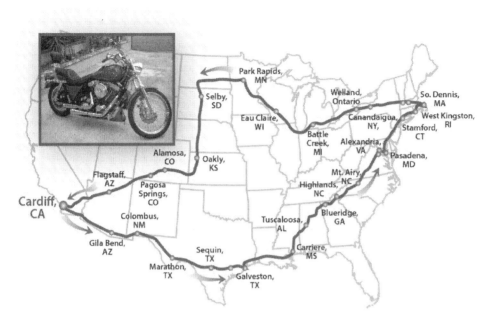

Map of route followed on this GREAT adventure!

Trip Statistics

- 42 days on the road.
- 32 Actual ride days.
- 8313 miles ridden.
- 32 states and 3 countries visited.
- Shortest ride – 65 miles.
- Longest ride – 511 miles.
- Average ride – 307 miles.
- Average mileage – 45 mpg.
- Average fuel cost – $2.98/Gal.
- Average motel cost – $56.00.
- Total cost of trip ~ $2300.00.
- Beers consumed ~ A bunch.
- About 83,130 MAGOTS monitored!

Trip Highlights

- Ruby ran and rode great.
- Spectacular wide-open vistas and scenery.
- Not much traffic on those "secondary" roads.
- Minimal weather issues.
- Scoped out lots of fishable rivers and streams.
- Plenty of early American history.
- Dozens of friendly and helpful folks met.
- Many friends and family visited.
- Successfully fended off one overly aggressive Mama San.
- Hundreds of friendly "salutes" from train engineers, roadside workers, truckers, chain gang prisoners and other bikers.

Part II - Bonus

The "Hardly Dangerous" Gang of Four Road Trip to Sturgis, SD
August 2 to 16, 2008

Riders:

Dean Mevis – Quality Assurance Manager, age 52 years.

> Nickname – Dean **"No sense of direction"** Mevis

Robert Booth – Director of Quality, age 60 years.

> Nickname – Bob **"Just call me your Black Jack Daddy, bitches"** Booth

Ron McDaniel – Quality Assurance Inspector, age 47 years.

> Nickname – Ron **"Rides the middle"** McDaniel

Steve Cook – Retired Oceanographer, age 63 years.

> Nickname – Steve **"No off road"** Cook (self tagged)

Six months before this trip, in February of 2008, after returning from a Scripps Institution of Oceanography cruise in the Indian Ocean I suffered a mild stroke. I was lucky in that minimal damage was incurred by me. I was still able to walk, talk, see, think and ride Ruby! One of my goals after buying Ruby was to make a Sturgis Motorcycle Rally run. Partnering up with this "Harly Dangerous" gang provided me with a bit of a support group to make the trip, even if they didn't know it.

Itinerary:

San Diego, CA to Wickenburg, AZ

Wickenburg, AZ to Grand Canyon National Park, AZ

Grand Canyon National Park, AZ to Monticello, UT

Monticello, UT to Steamboat Springs, CO

Steamboat Springs, CO to Wheatland, WY

Wheatland, WY to Rapid City, SD

Rapid City, SD to Hardin, MT

Hardin, MT to Moran, WY

Moran, WY to Evanston, WY

Evanston, WY to Henderson, NV

Henderson, NV to San Diego, CA

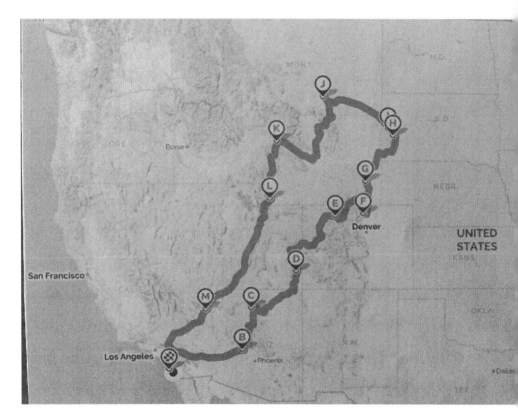

Route followed on this trip

August 2, 2008 - San Diego, CA to Wickenburg, AZ 372 Miles

Met up at the Tavern Rd. off ramp on US 8 at a gas station at 0700. Ron was waiting at a different gas station on the other side of the freeway. Bob called him and he found us. Dean kicked off the ride with a flask of Makers Mark bourbon that he shared with all of us. Headed east and stopped at a Denny's in El Centro for breakfast. Continued east to Yuma with the temperature rising higher and higher as the sun got higher and higher. Bob complained about my bike burning too rich and the exhaust bothered him so much that he decided not to follow me and passed me to ride in front of me. No worries as I don't mind riding drag, which I did for most of the trip anyway. Turned north toward Quartzite a bit east of Yuma. Gassed up in Quartzite with the temperature still rising. Quartzite is a shit hole and hot (110 degrees) as hell in August. Turned east at Quartzite headed toward Wickenburg. We stopped at every chance possible for gas and water. As I rode across the desert I could feel the heat reflecting off the asphalt highway, especially when I dropped into small arroyos. It felt like opening the door on a pottery kiln when it is burning full on. Dean chastised me for following too far back. He couldn't see me very well in his mirror. In fact I was following Bob as close as I could and it was he that maintained a large distance between himself and Ron who was following Dean. OK if Dean feels this way. As leader Dean is supposed to keep track of those behind him. Finally got to Wickenburg and the Best Western Grande Casa motel just in time as we were getting tired and heat fatigued. Too bad the pool was so cloudy with algae but that didn't stop Bob and Ron from enjoying it. When Bob would dive into the water he would completely disappear from sight. Bob got a bit drunk that night, I think, trying to compensate for the long ride and heat. We ate dinner at the Golden Nugget across the street from the motel. Also, had breakfast at the same place. Seemed to be the only show in town. Dean did a great job leading today as leading is always difficult.

August 3, 2008 - Wickenburg, AZ to the Grand Canyon, AZ 243 Miles

Late start as everyone slept in to recover from yesterday's ride. Finally got underway about 0900. Stopped in Prescott for a rest break and gas. Also stopped in Jerome for a beer break then headed off to Sedona. Bob and I got separated from Dean and Ron just outside Jerome. Dean was following his newly purchased GPS (which he followed religiously) and I was following the map. I think Dean would have followed that GPS over a cliff. Many attempts were made to contact via cell phone either Dean or Ron to meet up but were unsuccessful. Outside of Sedona Bob and I got caught in a thunderstorm that pretty much drenched us. There were many stops to put on rain gear and warmer cloths and attempted cell phone calls. Bob and I waited for Dean and Ron at a highway off ramp that we knew they would have to use just outside of Flagstaff. We saw them ride right by us without seeing us. We tried to chase them down but were unsuccessful. Bob was really getting pissed at Dean and Ron for not answering cell phone messages and returning our calls. We finally met up at the Grand Canyon Lodge at 1830 hours. Dean and Ron had already registered and were waiting outside for Bob and me to finally show up. That night we all kissed and made up although Dean again chastised me for not following the leader even though the leader went the wrong way. A pact was made that night to "ALWAYS" follow the leader or go my own way. We'll see how it goes tomorrow. Today can only be described as a cluster fuck.

Me at the Grand Canyon Overlook

August 4, 2008 - Grand Canyon, AZ to Monticello, UT 291 Miles

Depart Grand Canyon at 0900. Leaving the park we came to a T in the road that we were supposed to turn left and head east but Dean, again following his GPS, went right and started heading west (the wrong way). This was starting to get funny. As the roads were narrow it took me a few miles to pass everyone else and catch up to Dean. Just as I caught up to Dean he had already realized his mistake and was getting off the road at an overpass that would allow us to turn around and head east toward Cameron. When I finally caught up to him and the rest of the group I asked his if he was just "fucking" with me on purpose. He seriously said no and then we all started to go east (in the right direction). It turned out because I kept track for the rest of the trip, that every-time Dean came to a "T" in the road and the only choice was to go either right or left, he always went the wrong way. Really!

We all stopped a viewpoint that had a rocky parking lot and my boot slipped on the loose rocks and I dropped Ruby. Very embarrassing and it was a good thing those guys were there to help me right the bike. This is where my nickname "No off road" was born. It was a long hot day but the scenery was absolutely stunning as we rode through Monument Valley.

Later that afternoon we found the hard-to-find Running Iron Hotel 8 miles outside of Monticello. Finally met "Bob" the owner of the hotel. We (Bob Booth and myself) had talked on the phone with Running Iron Bob setting up this reservation. We had a great steak dinner that night and Bob let us have the run of the place. The next morning we made coffee, pulled the door shut behind us and departed. Our Bob couldn't get over how trusting Running Iron Hotel Bob was toward us. I think Bob has lived in the big cities too long and just hasn't met any rural folks with good judgment that really do trust people. He talked about him for days afterward to anyone who would listen including a breakfast waitress that was "enthralled" with his long discussion about Bob that kept her from her other paying and tipping customers.

Bob, me, Ron and Dean in front of the Running Iron Hotel

August 5, 2008 - Monticello, UT to Steamboat Springs, CO
392 Miles

Had breakfast in Moab, UT. Diverted from our route a few miles north of Moab to visit Arches National Park. Such spectacular rock formations, but only had time for a quick drive through and a few pictures. Would be better visited in the wintertime when the crowds would be lighter. After leaving Arches we basically rode up the Colorado River Valley all the way into Colorado again with very spectacular scenery. I wondered how much dynamite it took to blast that road out of those cliffs.

It was a beautiful ride along the river and saw many rafting groups headed downstream. Someday I would really like to raft the Colorado River and start way up here near the headwaters and eventually down into the Grand Canyon.

Worked our way up river toward Steamboat Springs and was redirected onto a country road by a gas station attendant to avoid construction and strict police in the town Oak Creek. Good idea as it was a nice and scenic little ride into Steamboat Springs.

August 6, 2008 - Steamboat Springs, CO to Wheatland, WY
310 Miles

Climbed over Milner Pass (10,759') and high point at Trail Ridge (12,183'). Pass still had snow at the top but we went over before noon and avoided any thunderstorm activity, which would have made for a very miserable ride. There must be at least 50% of the pine trees in the Rocky Mountain National Park infested with the Pine Bark Beetle. So many dead trees that it was not a very scenic run. Basically we were at the headwaters of the Colorado River. It was still a scenic view even with the dead trees. We stopped to visit Dean's sister (Heidi) in Fort Collins and she graciously feed us some lunch. We decided not to take the back roads but instead headed straight up I-25 to Wheatland to save some time. Had to deal with some wind issues upon reaching the flat plains of Wyoming.

Milner Pass, Colorado

August 7, 2008 - Wheatland, WY to Rapid City, SD 256 Miles

Mostly a lot of flatland here in Wyoming. Saw two female Pronghorn Antelope each with a set of twins. It must have been a good spring. More bikers starting to show up and the roads and gas stations are filling up with the sound of Harleys. Stopped by the Crazy Horse Monument, which is still under construction. A very impressive monument to our native indigenous people and should have been recognized as such over a hundred years ago. Construction funds all come from private donations which is why it is taking so long to complete. It cost $5.00 to get in and all the money goes toward the construction fund to complete it. Our government should contribute to this project to help speed it along to completion. I will probably never see it completed in my lifetime.

Stopped by Mt. Rushmore Memorial. Lot's of people there, met some nice folks, took a bunch of photos and then headed to Rapid City. This was a relatively short day as we got an early start this morning. Got settled into our motel, did laundry and cleaned the bike. Restaurant and bar right next door, so life is good. Weather is hot.

August 8, 2008 - Rapid City, SD to Sturgis, SD   97 Miles

Got to downtown Sturgis before 0900 and quickly found places to park, but not together. It was a mad house and we agreed that if we became separated that we would meet back at the bikes at noon. We quickly got separated, as I had to find a birthday card for Kathy and get it mailed. Also, had to say hello to the owner of the Broken Spoke Bar, Joe Bostard (an OTL acquaintance). Then had to look for an ex-Kraken employee who was supposed to be working at One Eyed Jacks, another crazy biker bar where all the female bartenders wore thongs or lingerie covered by biker leather chaps. All were very cute, I think. After a while, around mid afternoon, I returned to the bikes but the others had moved on. I had had enough and returned to the motel to go for a swim. Dean, Bob and Ron were not there. I think they went to the Full Throttle Bar for some beers. Turned out that they didn't and also hadn't moved their bikes but I never found them. While in Sturgis I purchased some fingerless gloves and a spare set of goggles. Had to buy

Got to downtown Sturgis before 0900 and quickly found places to park, but not together. It was a mad house and we agreed that if we became separated that we would meet back at the bikes at noon. We quickly got separated, as I had to find a birthday card for Kathy and get it mailed. Also, had to say hello to the owner of the Broken Spoke Bar, Joe Bostard (an OTL acquaintance). Then had to look for an ex-Kraken employee who was supposed to be working at One Eyed Jacks, another crazy biker bar where all the female bartenders wore thongs or lingerie covered by biker leather chaps. All were very cute, I think. After a while, around mid afternoon, I returned to the bikes but the others had moved on. I had had enough and returned to the motel to go for a swim. Dean, Bob and Ron were not there. I think they went to the Full Throttle Bar for some beers. Turned out that they didn't and also hadn't moved their bikes but I never found them. While in Sturgis I purchased some fingerless gloves and a spare set of goggles. Had to buy another Doo Rag and hat. I lost my hat earlier that morning on the ride in from Rapid City to Sturgis.

Downtown Sturges, South Dakota

Both Sturgis and Rapid City are jammed packed full of bikers and their trailers. Found my vest patch (**I rode mine - Sturgis 2008**) today and will have it sewed on tomorrow.

Bob, Dean, Myself and Ron at the 2008 Sturgis Motorcycle Rally

"The Hardly Dangerous Gang"

August 9, 2008 - Rapid City, SD to Deadwood, SD 58 Miles

Did a nice little solo loop from Rapid City to Deadwood to Sturgis then back to Rapid City. Came close to a doe and her fawn (still with its spots) just outside Deadwood. Deadwood is a cool little town but a bit touristy. The men are back in Sturgis but I decided to stay at the hotel and swim in the pool. Ron came back and did some laundry. Dean and Bob did a loop through Spearfish Canyon and just missed a serious thunderstorm.

My impression of the Sturgis Rally is that if you're into motorcycles then this is something that must be done. Many attend the rally but most trailer their bikes instead of riding them from home. I'm most proud of the patch I purchased for my vest. Plenty of chrome, accessories and proud women on display.

Sturgis Street entertainment

However, having been there, done that and bought the Tee Shirt, I don't need to go again. Just too crowded for me and I don't do crowds all that well.

The rest of the gang are still employed and used two weeks vacation time to do this Sturgis run. So, for most of this trip we've been on a tight schedule with not much room for "exploring." Consequently we will be leaving tomorrow to head home. Too bad, I would have liked to have lingered here and there a while.

August 10, 2008 - Rapid City, SD to Hardin, MT 282 Miles

Lots of rolling prairie and Pronghorn antelope along the way to Hardin. Good weather on the ride even though we could see a lot of afternoon thunderstorm activity in the mountains but none hit us. Stopped at the Little Bighorn National Monument where we met a nice couple from Sacramento (Gary and Rene Collum). Rene wanted my doo rag to use as a pattern to make one for Gary, so I gave it to her with strict instructions to boil it before touching it. Gary is a fly tier and will send me some later. He really liked my bike and told me he thought it had more "class" than the others. Stopped in Hardin Mt at the Lariat Motel, which was a real dump. We should have pressed on to Red Lodge.

Myself, Dean, Ron and Bob at the Little Big Horn National Monument

August 11, 2008 - Hardin, MT to Moran, WY 320 Miles

Rode over the Beartooth Mountain Range and pass at over 10,000 feet. It was cold and windy with lots of 15mph curves and very scenic. Dropped down into Yellowstone National Park and visited Old Faithful. Once again it was a fast drive by and I would like to spend more time visiting which I will do when Kathy retires. Lost a headlamp so we stopped in Billings MT at a Napa auto parts store. Dean jumped to it and found the right parts and repaired it in short time. Although I was later blamed for making us late for our arrival at the Flagg Ranch resort after a long and arduous day with lots of traffic. Better to visit Yellowstone in the off-season. Stayed in cabins at the Flagg Ranch and had dinner at the lodge. Only problem was there was no bartender and the food was cold.

Hardly Dangerous Gang in the Yellowstone Valley

August 12, 2008 - Moran, WY to Evanston, WY 256 Miles

Cold morning so we waited until the sun rose and was up for a while. Stopped at Jenny Lake for a photo op. Saw some Pronghorn antelope and one real nice buck. Arrived in Evanston and it was hot. We checked into the Howard Johnson's but it did not have a pool and that bothered Bob a lot. However, I think he found some solace in the hot tube, especially after I brought him a double "Black Jack". Good bar and restaurant and the bartender took great care of us. I ate by myself at the bar and met up with the others later.

Jenny Lake, Wyoming

August 13, 2008 - Evanston, WY to Henderson, NV 535 Miles

Once again became separated from the others approaching Provo UT. Our target was the Harley Davidson Dealership in Provo but when I reached the "T" in the highway Provo was to the left and the others, too far ahead of me to see, had turned right following Dean's GPS. I stopped at a 7/11 and unsuccessfully tried to get directions to the Harley dealership. I kept going south following the original itinerary but never found the others. I was getting tired of the ride and it was obvious that I was just slowing everyone else down so when I saw the I-15 south headed toward Las Vegas I "smelled" San Diego and decided to head for home. This would mean that I didn't get to Zion National Park and gave up two extra nights on the road. I called everyone and left a message about my decision but was only able to talk to Ron. Climbed over another 10,000 foot pass and basically followed the Bear River. Kept feeling OK so I called my cousins Terri and Randy in Henderson and asked if I could stay the night with them. Arrived about 1900 that evening. I called Kathy to wish her a Happy Birthday.

August 14, 2008 - Henderson, NV to Cardiff, CA 318 Miles

Had a great steak dinner at Randy and Terri's place, re-hydrated with tons of water and three beers, watched a little of the Olympics then crashed. Early the next morning Randy and I had some quiet time on the patio sipping coffee. Randy is really a nice guy, very warm and engaging. They fixed bacon and eggs, biscuits and watermelon for breakfast. Prior to leaving Terri took a few photos of me on Ruby and sent them home via email. The pictures got home before I did. A few months later, at a family reunion, Terri surprised me with a painting she did of me sitting on Ruby. It was great and a fine reminder of this great trip and she even captured my Masonic ring that belonged to my father.

Left early to try and avoid as much road heat as possible but it was still a long day of brutal heat reflecting off the asphalt highway and I had to stop in Baker, Barstow and a rest area just to re-wet my Doo Rag and scarf. Was grateful to finally begin to feel some cooling at Victorville with the ocean air coming over the Cajon Grade. Arrived home about 1700 hours.

Teri's painting

Trip Highlights

Beginning mileage: 46,851 miles.
Ending mileage: 50,572 miles.
Total miles ridden: 3,721 miles.
About 75 gallons of fuel used ~ 49 mpg.
Thirteen days on the road.
Longest ride was 535 miles.
Shortest ride was 58 miles (just around Sturgis)
Average ride day was 287 miles.
Scored on "I rode mine - Sturgis 2008" patch.

One year after (2009) this Sturgis ride having done everything I wanted to do with a motorcycle I sold Ruby after riding her more than 20,000 miles. **Loved every mile!**

Personal Details:

Beginning mileage: 46,851

Ending mileage: 50,572

Total miles ridden: 3721 miles

About 75 gallons of fuel used = ~49 mpg

Made in the USA
Monee, IL
04 September 2019